A

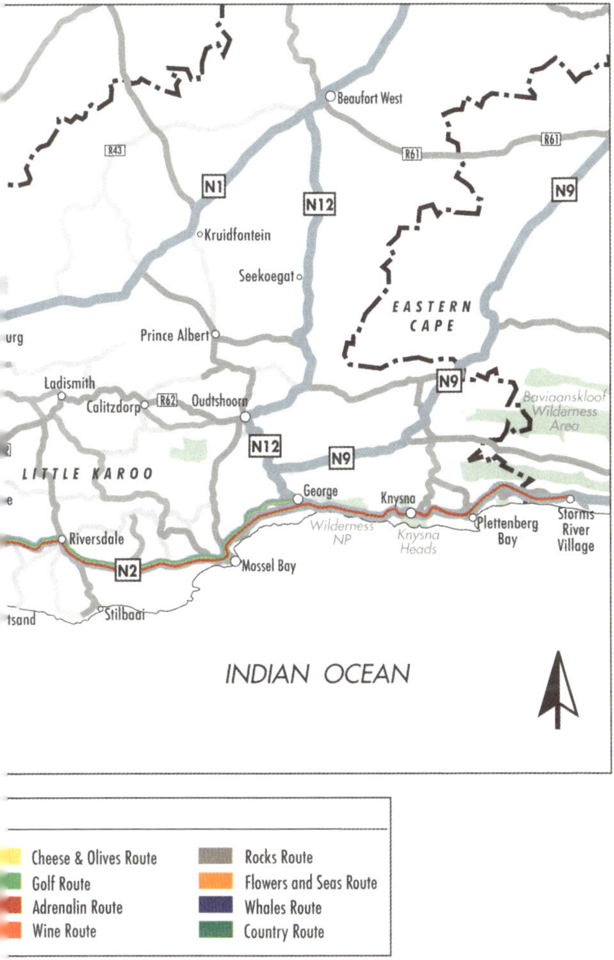

○Beaufort West

R43

N1

N12

R61   R61

N9

○Kruidfontein

Seekoegat○

EASTERN
CAPE

urg

Prince Albert○

Ladismith
○

Calitzdorp○   R62   Oudtshoorn○

N9

Baviaanskloof
Wilderness
Area

LITTLE KAROO

N12   **N9**

○George   Knysna

e

Wilderness
NP

Knysna
Heads

○Plettenberg
Bay

Storms
River
Village

2

○Riversdale

N2

○Mossel Bay

tsand   ○Stilbaai

INDIAN OCEAN

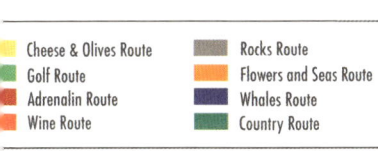

▭ Cheese & Olives Route	▭ Rocks Route
▭ Golf Route	▭ Flowers and Seas Route
▭ Adrenalin Route	▭ Whales Route
▭ Wine Route	▭ Country Route

THE

CAPE

Route Finder

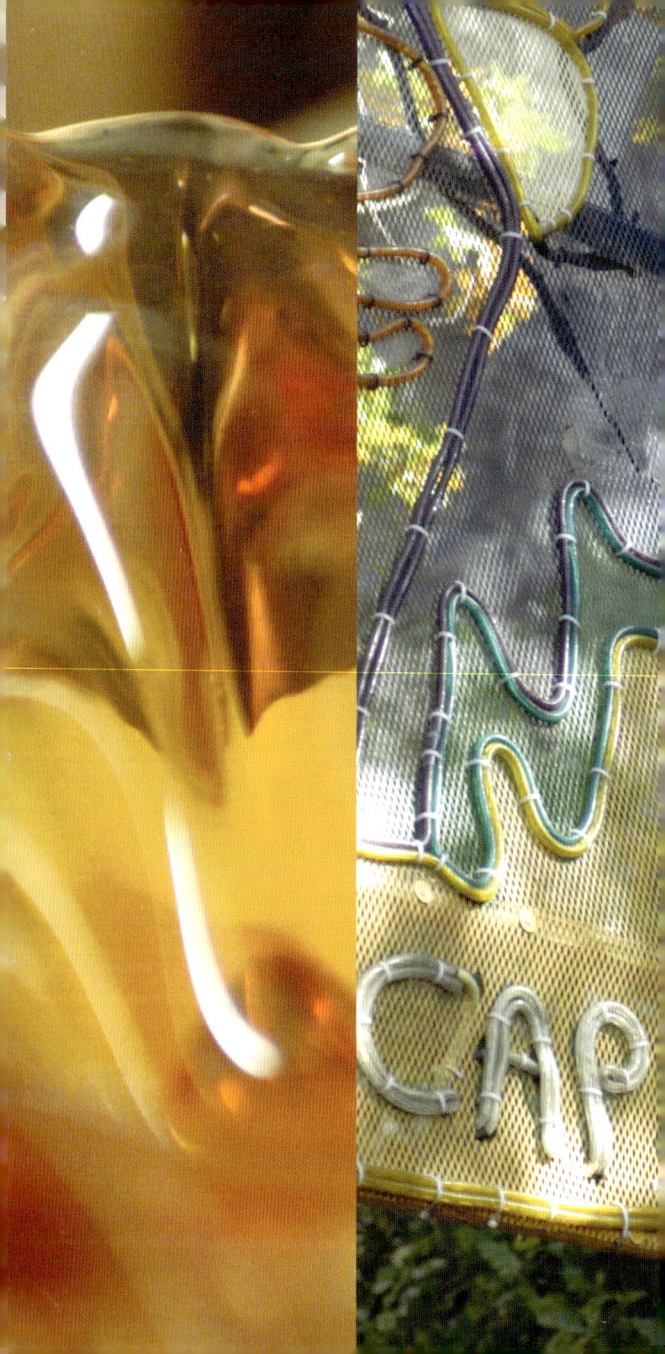

THE
CAPE
Route Finder

ADÉLLE HORLER

First published in 2004 by Struik Publishers
(a division of New Holland Publishing (South Africa) (Pty) Ltd)
New Holland Publishing is a member of Johnnic Communications Ltd

London • Cape Town • Sydney • Auckland

Cornelis Struik House, 80 McKenzie Street, Cape Town 8001

ISBN 1 86872 943 5

1 3 5 7 9 10 8 6 4 2

Publishing Manager: Dominique le Roux
Managing Editor: Lesley Hay-Whitton
Designers: Sian Marshall and Illana Fridkin
Editors: Erika Bornman and Michelle Coburn
Proofreader: Tessa Kennedy
Indexer: Mary Lennox

Reproduction by Hirt & Carter Cape (Pty) Ltd
Printed and bound by Sing Cheong Printing Company Limited

DISCLAIMER
While every effort has been made to ensure accuracy, the author and the
publisher will not be liable for any inconvenience or loss resulting from possible
inaccuracies. Information such as telephone numbers, email addresses, roads
and maps could have changed since the authors researched the routes, and the
publisher would appreciate updated information. Please write to:
The Editor, Great Cape Route Finder, PO Box 1144, Cape Town, 8000 or email
updates@struik.co.za

www.imagesofafrica.co.za

IMAGES OF AFRICA
PHOTO LIBRARY

CONTENTS

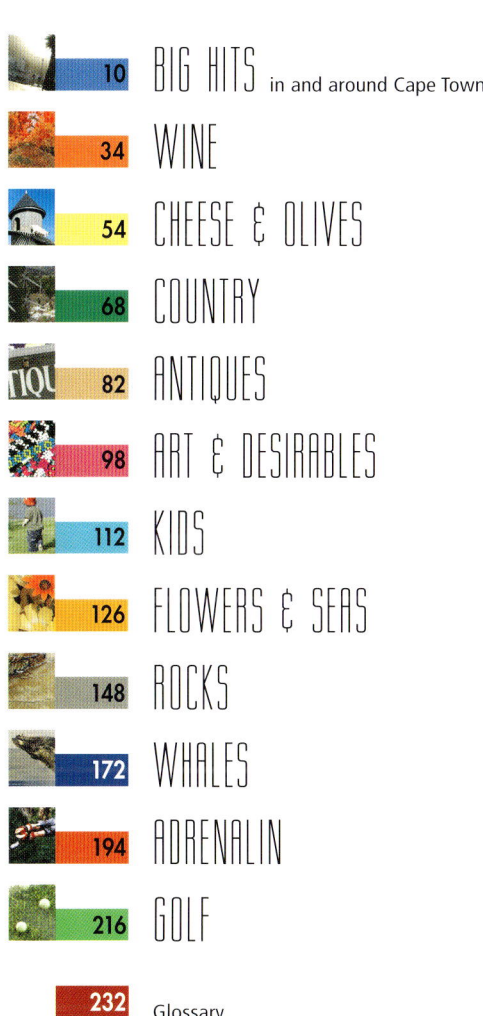

The author

Adélle Horler is a travel writer and expedition guide who's lucky enough to live in a region that has so many stories to tell. Former managing editor of lifestyle guides *Drive Out*, *Eat Out*, *Eat In* and *Sleep Over*, Adélle freelances for various magazines, happily indulging her desire to head off whenever something new and exciting appears on the horizon.

Author acknowledgements

For their input and advice, thank you to Larry Gould, Myrna Robins, Jenny Morris, Les Spiro, Lindsaye MacGregor, Stu Hermansen and Peter Slingsby. For patience and enthusiasm, thanks to the top team at Struik – Dominique le Roux, Erika Bornman, Sian Marshall and Illana Fridkin. And especially to Vivien Horler for her 'hedgehog' eye, and Geoff Dalglish, travelling companion on all sorts of paths.

PLEASE NOTE

The starting point for all the routes is the intersection between the main entrance to the V&A Waterfront, and the Cape Town International Convention Centre, where the highway, Table Bay Boulevard, becomes Buitengracht and crosses Coen Steytler Avenue.

COLL-LOCAL-ISMS

South African English isn't always as it sounds

Circle: roundabout

Lekker: great, sweet, lovely, delicious

Robot: a traffic light

Now: imminently

Now-now: in a little while

Just now: not for a while (also 'a while ago')

ON THE ROAD

Road signs in Afrikaans often bear little resemblance to the English, as in *Kaapstad* (Cape Town) and *Langstraat* (Long Street). *Slaggate* are potholes, and *stadig* is a caution to go slowly.

For your own sanity, avoid the major routes in and out of the city centre in peak traffic periods. These extend from about 7:30 to 9:30 in the mornings towards the city and 16:30 to 18:30 in the evenings leaving the city.

Another good thing to know, especially on highways between towns, is that local drivers tend to pull over onto the road shoulder to allow you to pass. This isn't strictly legal but it helps, especially when you're behind big trucks. The gracious thing is to say thanks by flashing your hazard lights or raising your hand in front of the rear view mirror. If an oncoming car flashes their lights, they're probably warning of a speed trap ahead. Speed limits vary from 60km/h to 80km/h in built-up areas, increasing to 100km/h and 120km/h on the open freeways.

You'll encounter 'car guards', formal and informal, in almost every town. They'll watch your parked car for a tip, anything from R1 to R5, more if you're feeling generous.

A couple of the routes in this book include stretches of gravel road. These roads are good and safe – simply reduce your speed and avoid the loose stones at the road sides, where it's easy to skid. When approaching a corner, slow down while still on the straight, so you're not braking as you turn.

Please note that odometer readings vary from one vehicle to another, so use mileages in the route directions as a guide. Unless directed otherwise, zero your odometer as you leave each venue.

UPFRONT

Where else can you watch the sun rise and set over the sea, and swim in two different oceans – all on the same day? How many other cities in the world have a nature reserve at their heart?

But of course you know the Western Cape has lots of good stuff – that's why you're here. The question is, where do you start?

To cut through the bewildering array of options facing visitors, we gathered the advice of a varied bunch of *Kapenaars* and put together 12 specific routes, each around a theme. So this is what locals believe you mustn't miss on a visit to the Cape (and hopefully it'll also remind residents that there are plenty of tempting reasons to be a tourist on our own doorstep).

Whether you're South African or come from across the sea, this is touring made easy as we've done the planning for you. All you need do is pick a route and get behind the wheel. The 12 routes have been designed to overlap, so you can link them together or create your own, and there's a mix of day trips, weekends and longer breakaways to suit all itineraries.

So think of The Cape Route Finder as your personal tour guide, one that won't get grumpy if you suddenly decide to stay longer, or change routes altogether. However you use it, have fun and then come back for more – you're always guaranteed a warm Cape welcome.

Adélle

Simon's Town Main Road at dawn

THE ROUTE:
With just a couple of days in the Mother City, here's everything you *have* to see, from Table Mountain to Cape Point and all the good stuff in between.

see MAPS A & B

contact details on pp 32 & 33

TIME: Two days

DISTANCE: Under 30km on Day One, and 120km on Day Two

BEST TIME TO GO: No matter the season, the city welcomes you all year. The beaches are packed in summer's heat, tempered by blustery days thanks to the Cape's notorious Southeaster. Winter's become known as the secret season, when rainy days punctuate halcyon spells of sunny weather. But being Cape Town's weatherman is no easy task – the city has a reputation for dishing up four seasons all in one day.

big hits

INTRODUCTION

If you have only a day or two in Cape Town, this route covers the greatest hits, all the stuff you really have to do if you want to say you've seen the Mother City. Capetonians can be very smug. As someone once said, they know they've got it, others want it, and sometimes they don't really feel like sharing. So now you don't have to ask – here's a summary of the best Cape Town has to offer. Of course there's plenty more to do – whenever the route zips close to an attraction that's really worthwhile, it gets a lightning mention so you can go back and explore at your leisure. Here's hoping the Mother rocks you.

READING LIST

✓ *Time Out Cape Town*, sister magazine to the London version, is packed with comprehensive listings on what to do and see in the city.

✓ *Cape Town – Don't Tell*, written by Sam Woulidge and Sheryl Ozinsky (Struik), blows the whistle on all the places Capetonians would rather keep secret.

✓ The Kalk Bay Historical Association has produced two fascinating booklets on the history and buildings from Muizenberg to the bay. These are great to use if you're exploring on foot.

Jazz African-style

Chapman's Peak Drive is one of the most spectacular along the South African coast

THE ROUTE

Day One

- See Greenmarket Square and the city centre
- Watch the 62 300th firing (or thereabouts) of the Noon Gun
- See the city from Signal Hill
- Take the cableway to lunch on Table Mountain
- Catch the ferry to Robben Island
- Dine African style or take a township jazz tour

Day Two

- Breakfast at Kirstenbosch National Botanical Garden
- Stop for a tasting on the Constantia Wine Route
- Look for whales from Boyes Drive to Kalk Bay
- Laugh at the penguins on Boulders Beach
- Lunch in Simon's Town (or Cape Point or Scarborough)
- See the end of the African continent at Cape Point
- Drive along the Atlantic Seaboard and Chapman's Peak Drive
- Have a sundowner picnic on the beach

BEFORE YOU GO

- ✓ In peak season, December–January, allow extra time in traffic, particularly along the Atlantic Seaboard (Camps Bay through Clifton and Sea Point) and False Bay from Muizenberg to Simon's Town.

- ✓ The timing can be quite tight for Robben Island in the afternoon, as the last boat for the day leaves at 15:00. (You can make the 3.5hr trip in the morning, but won't be back in time for the Noon Gun.) Otherwise, spend longer on the mountain, and do the island another day.

- ✓ If the Kirstenbosch concerts are on (from December to March, Sundays at 17:30), you may want to do Day Two in reverse, ending with a picnic at the concert.

- ✓ Some of the estates on the Constantia Wine Route are closed on Sundays, so be sure to check opening times.

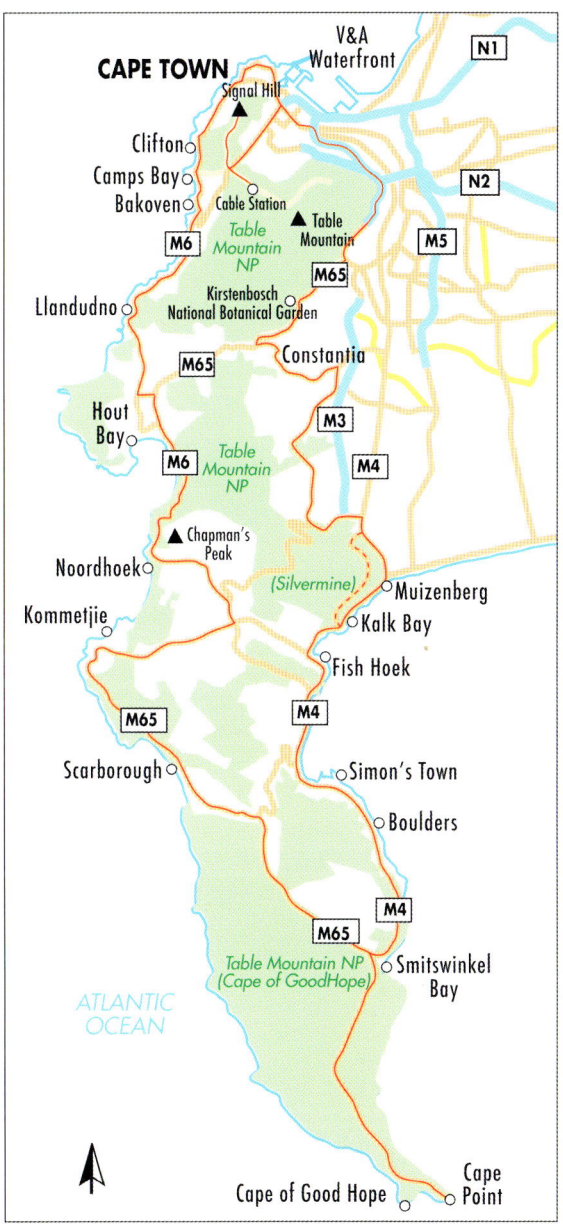

Table Mountain reflected in a pond in the Company's Garden

ONE

Waterfront to Riebeeck Square – 5min

From the Waterfront turn right into Buitengracht (M62 Camps Bay), following cableway signs. At almost 1km turn left into Kortmark (Shortmarket Street) and park on Riebeeck Square – fee payable.

You can't soak up the soul of a city from inside a car, so get out and up close to the people, with a few hours on foot. Heritage Square, with its interesting shopping and good restaurants, is right across the road.

Otherwise, a wander down Shortmarket Street will bring you to Greenmarket Square, a bustling curio market on every day of the week, where farmers once brought fruit and vegetables for sale. The Old Town House dominates the square. When proclamations were read from the balcony, the people of Cape Town were summoned by the bell on the roof. Today, the Old Town House is home to a display of Dutch and Flemish art, and you can grab a cup of tea and bite to eat in the leafy courtyard.

There are more curio stalls, street musicians and pavement cafés up St George's Mall, with the graceful St George's Cathedral (over which Nobel Peace Prize winner Archbishop Desmond Tutu presided) at the top, on the edge of the Company's Garden. The latter, an oasis of green calm, birdsong and squirrels, was originally planted to supply passing ships by the first Dutch governor of the Cape, Jan van Riebeeck, in 1652. From the Slave Lodge, built to house the slaves who worked in the Company's Garden and now a museum, stroll up Government Avenue past Parliament to the SA National Gallery (with the

CAPE TOWN'S BEST

✓ for sundowners – Table Mountain; Clifton Fourth Beach or Camps Bay beach (in fact any of the Atlantic Seaboard beaches); or La Med if you like the bar scene.

✓ for afternoon tea – take high tea at the Mount Nelson and feel like a true colonial, or at the Table Bay Hotel in the Waterfront, looking at the water and Table Mountain.

✓ for full moon – walk up Lion's Head and watch the sunset and moonrise from the top. (It's generally light enough to see your way down, but take a torch. And a bottle of wine.)

✓ for quirky shopping – wander up Long Street for a mix of history, architecture, on-the-edge fashion and off-beat locals, or check out De Waterkant's super-cool chic.

✓ for concerts – the summer sunset concert season at Kirstenbosch, every Sunday from December to March at 17:30, where you take a picnic and watch from the lawns; or head to Stellenbosch for Spier's starlight concerts – have dinner, then stroll to the amphitheatre.

✓ for meeting the community – do the Cape Care Route, a Trail of Two Cities, which showcases projects where people care for the planet and each other. Meet emerging entrepreneurs, impoverished women who are building their own homes, and youths who are creating art out of discarded waste.

Jewish Museum and Holocaust Centre behind it) and the SA Museum and Planetarium. If you cross St George's Mall you can wander down Adderley Street, where great old colonial buildings rub shoulders with modern malls. Walk past the flower sellers in Trafalgar Place, or turn into Darling Street to take you to the City Hall (which contains a huge organ with 3 165 pipes). Cross the Grand Parade to the Castle of Good Hope, built in the shape of a five-pointed star, which vies with the Posthuys in Muizenberg as South Africa's oldest European building.

Alternatively, from the parking area walk up Buitengracht and turn right into Wale Street to explore the colourful buildings of the Bo-Kaap (Upper Cape), the birthplace of Islam in South Africa, and home to many residents who can trace their ancestors back to slaves of the Cape Colony. At New Year, especially Tweede Nuwe Jaar (Second New Year, 2 January, a Cape Town peculiarity – it was the only day slaves had off for the entire year!), the Bo-Kaap is a riot of colour and sound as the Kaapse Klopse, or Cape Minstrel bands, sing and dance their way between crowds of onlookers. The Bo-Kaap Museum is at 71 Wale Street.

Wherever you go, be back at the car by about 11:30, to get to the firing of the Noon Gun (it waits for no-one).

Riebeeck Square to Lion Battery – 5min
Turn left back onto Buitengracht. After 500m turn right into Bloem Street (signed for Noon Gun) and immediately left into Jordaan. The road curves right twice, then at about 1km turn left into Whitford, which becomes Military Road. Keep straight to the battery at just over 2km.

Garbage and graffiti make the route to the battery look dodgy, but proceed in good faith. You'll be rewarded by gorgeous views

BE YOUR OWN WEATHERMAN
No matter how perfect the day, if there's a small puff of cloud perched on the top of Lion's Head, rain is on its way.

Sunrise as seen from Rhodes Memorial

of the City Bowl, and a living piece of history. There are several guns up here – 21-gun salutes to visiting ships erupt from this battery – but the 18-pounder Noon Gun tops them all (there are actually two, used alternately, and both are loaded in case one misfires). They were originally fired so that ships in the bay could synchronise their chronometers, and now... well, because we like it. The tradition goes back to 1806 – they've been fired every day (except Sundays), so they're now well past 62 000 bangs. You can watch them being loaded – with 1.5 kilograms of gun powder in cloth bags – then join the countdown. Blocking your ears is highly recommended.

If you want to look like a local, remember that the firing of the Noon Gun instantly separates tourists from Capetonians. As the gun booms out over the city, visitors (jumpy about South African crime) stare wildly about, while Capetonians look at their watches. So if you want to look like you belong, next time you hear the gun, be cool and check the time.

Lion Battery to Signal Hill viewsite – 15min

Retrace the route from the battery. Keep straight down Whitford Road at 1.2km. Turn left at the bottom, then right and right again into Buitengracht. Follow M62 Camps Bay and brown cableway signs to the intersection at 4.5km. Turn right into Signal Hill Drive and follow it to the parking area.

Mind the tour buses that toil along this road and tend to park rather awkwardly on the corners, but they're also enjoying the awesome views of the City Bowl hugged by Table Mountain, and round to Robben Island, Sea Point and Green Point, with the Atlantic Ocean sparkling to the horizon.

And now, if you don't feel you're high enough already – prepare to fly...

Signal Hill to Table
Mountain Lower Cableway – 5min

Leave the viewsite and return to intersection. Go 'straight' across to Tafelberg Road, which winds up to the Lower Cable Station at 4km. The ancient San people, or Bushmen, called Table Mountain *Hoerikwaggo* (Mountain of the Sea) as it rises from the low-lying Cape Flats, which used to be underwater, and soars to a majecstic 1 085 metres at Maclear's Beacon.

No-one will ever take you seriously again if you come to Cape Town and don't stand on top of the Table. So get in line (inconveniently, they don't take bookings, so allow about half an hour for queuing) and buy your ticket for the aerial cableway – definitely the easiest way up. The ride takes just under five minutes, and the car rotates so that the panorama changes from city to sea to mountain. It goes without saying that the 360-degree views of Table Bay, False Bay, Robben Island and the Peninsula from the top are spectacular – just mind you don't trip over a dassie while you're staring out to sea.

Explore the paths that criss-cross the summit, and end at the fully licensed restaurant (or settle down for a picnic with the best view in town). If you're up for the ultimate adrenalin fix, try the 112-metre abseil over Camps Bay, see Adrenalin Route, p 200.

Table Mountain to
Waterfront for Robben Island – 20min

Leave the Lower Cable Station and return to the intersection. Go 'straight' across to Kloof Road (between the Camps Bay road and Signal Hill Drive). At the 2.1km T-junction turn right into Lower Kloof Road. At 4.3km turn left into Queens Road and keep straight to the sea, then through Sea Point on Beach Road, with the sea on your left. At 7.5km keep straight to the city. Go straight across the traffic circle at Green Point. At 10.2km turn left onto Buitengracht (brown sign to CTICC). Turn into the Waterfront to the Clock Tower and Robben Island tours. (If you're running late for the boat, take the direct route back down Buitengracht to the Waterfront.)

The high point of the Robben Island tour is the cell where apartheid prisoner-turned-president Nelson Mandela spent almost two decades of his life. And the list of inmates who shared the other cells in that passage is astonishing — it reads a bit like a who's who of South Africa's first democratic government.

It's a good idea to book in advance, but bear in mind the tour is weather permitting. Get your tickets at the Nelson Mandela Gateway close to the Clock Tower, or you can book over the phone with a credit card. Before you board, make time to view the museum on the history of the island and the political struggle. The ferry trip to the island takes about 25 minutes.

Your guide will be a former political prisoner, and the tour includes a drive around the island, where you can get great photos of Table Mountain.

After the boat trip back to the Waterfront, discuss the events of the day over dinner. Taste the foods of the entire continent at Africa Café on Heritage Square – simply retrace this morning's route and park on Riebeeck Square. Or tour the townships to the beat of drums and traditional African instruments on a Township Music Tour.

TWO

Waterfront to Kirstenbosch Botanical Garden – 10min

From the Waterfront, turn left onto N1 Paarl, then N2 Somerset West, M3 Muizenberg. At about 5km keep right at Hospital Bend, following M3 Muizenberg and brown signs to Kirstenbosch. At about

A Sunday summer sunset concert at Kirstenbosch

10km, turn right at traffic lights into Rhodes Drive, M63 Hout Bay and Kirstenbosch. Turn right into the gardens at 12km.

This is the only place you'll see a baobab in the Western Cape, towering over a conservatory of desert plants and succulents, with a forest of cycads and a fern garden next door. But the main event here in Kirstenbosch, one of the 'Seven Magnificent Botanical Gardens of the World', is the fabulous setting of manicured lawns and beautiful beds of flowers giving way to natural vegetation sweeping up to the towering mountain above. This isn't a stuffy outing for gardeners only – it's an abundantly beautiful and peaceful place where the kids can zoom around while you enjoy breakfast in the sun. There's also a Braille Trail, a Fragrance Garden, a Useful Plants Garden, a Water-wise Garden, as well as several restaurants, a nursery and a shop.

En route on the M3 to Kirstenbosch you'll pass:

- Groote Schuur Hospital, on your left, where the world's first heart transplant was performed by surgeon Chris Barnard in 1967. There is now a Transplant Museum in the theatre where the operation was performed.
- Mostert's Mill, a little further on the left, is a fully restored Dutch windmill built in 1796 and a reminder that all this land was once farmland, with grain stored in the Groote Schuur (Great Barn), after which the hospital is named.
- Rhodes Memorial, on your right, is a rather grand granite monument to Cecil John Rhodes, whose vision was to snap up most of Africa for the glory of the British Empire. On his death, he bequeathed all this land (later occupied by the University of Cape Town and Kirstenbosch) to the nation.

LIVING HISTORY

At Kirstenbosch you can still see part of a wild almond hedge planted by Jan van Riebeeck in 1660.

Kirstenbosch to Constantia Wine Route – 10–20min (depending where you stop)

Turn right back onto Rhodes Drive, then T-junction right to Hout Bay and Constantia Nek. At Constantia Nek circle (5km) turn sharp left to Constantia Main Road (M41 Wynberg). The turning to Groot Constantia is at about 8km. At about 9.5km turn right at traffic lights into Ladies Mile Road (M39 Bergvliet). At next lights (10.5km) turn right onto M42 Tokai. Follow the Constantia Wine Route signs to Buitenverwachting and Klein Constantia, and later Constantia Uitsig. At 15km go straight through the circle. The entrance to Steenberg Wine and Golf Estate is at the second circle at 16km.

Unless you're a seriously quick drinker, you'll have to pick just one or two of the estates along the Constantia Wine Route, and it's not an easy choice.

These estates were the first to produce wine in South Africa, which was enjoyed in the eighteenth century by European royals, Napoleon and even gains mention in Jane Austen's *Sense and Sensibility*. All estates have award-winning wines available for tasting in beautiful settings.

Constantia Wine Route to Penguins at Boulders – 35min

Continue from Steenberg Estate circle and go straight through several traffic lights. At 3km, T-junction right into Main Road M4 Muizenberg, brown sign to Cape Point. After about 600m, turn right onto Boyes Drive for fantastic views over Zandvlei, Muizenberg and False Bay to Kalk Bay.

From Boyes Drive, look out for whales in the bay from August to October. An alternative route is to keep straight on Main Road and not turn right to Boyes Drive. Although there's usually more traffic, it takes you along the seafront through St James to Kalk Bay. The grand stone houses that line this road make it easy to see why this used to be called 'millionaire's mile' – many were built by wealthy mining magnates who made their money from the gold and diamond rushes.

On Main Road, look out for Rhodes's Cottage, bought by Cecil John in 1899, and where he died at just 49 years of age. (There is a cigar burn on one of the tables that's said to have

DID YOU KNOW?

The African penguins at Boulders have the ability to make the most grumpy among us smile. Always well dressed in tuxedos, the white feathers underneath is camouflage for underwater predators, with the black on top for predators from above. They mate for life and take turns to sit on eggs and feed their chicks. But as sweet as that sounds, don't be too fooled – they pack a mean bite.

been made by former British Prime Minister Winston Churchill.) A little further on lies The Posthuys, a building that possibly predates the Castle as the earliest European building in the Cape, as it is thought to have been built in 1673, a whole year before the Castle was completed.

Stop at one of the popular places Capetonians won't easily tell you about – the Olympia Café opposite the harbour at Kalk Bay – for delectable pastries and a friendly buzz. (Turn left onto Main Road from Boyes Drive and park in the street or at the harbour.) Kalk Bay itself is also well worth a wander. (See the Antiques Route, pp 93–95.)

After 10km, Boyes Drive curves left down to the T-junction with Main Road – turn right and drive through Clovelly and Fish Hoek. At 13km turn left at the circle to Simon's Town, and travel next to the sea past Glencairn and through Simon's Town. You can either turn left at about 22km into Seaforth Road, at the brown sign to the penguins, or go a little further and turn left into Bellevue Road, signed for penguins and Boulders Beach.

The main penguin viewing area is from Seaforth – there's a restaurant, curio stalls and a shop, with boardwalks taking you through nesting areas to a platform on the beach. But if you

fancy something slightly quieter, with a chance actually to get your feet into sand and sea, go to Boulders Beach. (Entrance fee charged at both places.)

There's a restaurant and gift shop before you walk down to a tiny beach that all but disappears at high tide. Here humans and penguins share the sand, and the swimming is fabulous – flat and calm, amid huge 540-million-year-old boulders. A wheelchair friendly path behind the beach takes you all the way to the Seaforth side, so you can still see the breeding areas. Just check underneath your car before you leave – some penguins might be enjoying a bit of shade.

Penguins to Cape Point – 20min (to park entrance)

Leave Seaforth parking area and turn left into Main Road.
After 10km turn left into Cape of Good Hope Nature Reserve.
The restaurant is a further 12km from the gate.

Here's where the continent of Africa tapers to a rugged, rocky point, and currents clash to create wild seas that lash the land, prompting explorer Bartolomeu Dias to call it Cabo Tormentoso, Cape of Storms, in 1488. Portugal's King John II, possibly Cape Town's first public relations officer, later changed it to Cape of Good Hope, which is used today. Things got even better in 1580 when Sir Francis Drake described it as 'the fairest Cape we saw in the whole circumference of the earth'.

You could spend the entire day here – there are endless hikes that will reward with fantastic vistas, whales, birdlife, richly diverse fynbos and game if you're lucky. The Chacma baboons are said to be the only ones in the world to have developed a taste for seafood. (Keep your distance as they can be dangerous, and definitely don't feed them. Keep car windows and doors closed if they're nearby, and back off slowly if a baboon approaches you.)

You can picnic and swim at one of several beaches or tidal pools, or explore the history of the place, from San hunter gatherers who lived among these rocks, to early global explorers who landed here (Dias and Da Gama erected crosses). Stories of numerous wrecks abound, including the famous *Lusitania*

HUNGRY YET?

If you want to avoid the tour buses in Simon's Town or Cape Point, hold out for Scarborough (about 15 minutes from Cape Point), to eat at Cobbs at the Cape or Camel Rock restaurant.

which went down off the Point in 1911, and the *Flying Dutchman*, the subject of Wagner's famous opera, which sank in 1680, her captain vowing to round the Cape if it took him till Doomsday. He's still trying, they say — the ghostly galleon has been sighted through the fog on many an occasion, including by Britain's King George V.

But this is a quick visit, so take the funicular for a brief ride up to the old lighthouse, and if you like a walk on the wild side, stroll down to the working lighthouse right at the Point, just 87 metres above the crashing surf.

Cape Point via Scarborough to Chapman's Peak Drive – 50min without the stop-over for lunch)

Turn left onto M65 for Scarborough, past curio stands. (Cape Point Ostrich Farm is on your right.) At 8km turn left,

Something for everyone in Kalk Bay

DID YOU KNOW?

Because of its pure air, Cape Point is the site of a Global Atmosphere Watch Station, one of only 20 in the world. It's a research laboratory that monitors long-term changes in the chemistry of the earth's atmosphere, looking at solar radiation and ozone and methane trace gases, that may impact upon the climate.

following M65. Enter Scarborough at about 10km, with Camel Rock on your left at 11km, and the two Scarborough restaurants immediately after it. Keep straight at the 4-way stop (16km) and enter Kommetjie at about 18km. Pass Imhoff Farm at 22km and Solele Game Reserve at 25km. At 26.5km, turn left at traffic lights to M65, Ou Kaapse Weg (Old Cape Road). At 27.5km, turn left at traffic lights to M6 Noordhoek. Pass Noordhoek Farm Village (stop for tea!) at 31km. Chapman's Peak Drive toll road starts 500m later. Settle back for a lazy return drive towards town, along a route that's been described as the most beautiful in the world. And there's a sunset picnic at the end of it. The route starts amid natural fynbos before skirting the sea again at Scarborough. Misty Cliffs is an idyllic cluster of houses before the road drops down past Slangkop lighthouse into Kommetjie. Yes, those are camels at Imhoff Farm. Dip inland briefly before climbing above Noordhoek's endless beach to Chapman's Peak Drive, an

awesome marine road carved out of the mountain with sheer, boulder-strewn drops to the sea. (A toll fee is charged.)

Chapman's Peak Drive to Llandudno, Bakoven, Camps Bay or Clifton Fourth Beach. (Llandudno – 25min, Bakoven – 30min, Camps Bay – 35min, Clifton Fourth – 40min)

After leaving Chapman's Peak, drive through Hout Bay. At the second traffic circle (42km) turn left to M6 Llandudno. (Pass Valley Road to World of Birds at 43km.) At the next traffic lights turn right to Llandudno. For Llandudno beach, turn left at 45km. For Bakoven turn left into Beta Road at about 52km. Pass Balie Bay at 53km and enter Camps Bay. Pass left to La Med, then turn left to The Ridge and Clifton Fourth Beach at 55km.

Chapman's Peak Drive delivers you to Hout Bay (which not so long ago declared itself an independent republic!) and then it's a fabulously scenic drive to a variety of perfect sundowner spots. Take your pick from Llandudno, where there might still be time to catch some tanning rays; Bakoven, where you can grab a quick swim or sit among the seagulls on the rocks; Camps Bay's wide open spaces; or Clifton Fourth Beach – good if there's a bit of a breeze. If you don't feel like a picnic, take your pick of Camps Bay's back-to-back pavement cafés and trendy restaurants.

29

Clifton Fourth Beach to Waterfront – 20min

From the turn to Clifton Fourth, continue through Bantry Bay, turn left into Seacliffe at 2.2km. Go along the beachfront through Sea Point and Three Anchor Bay. Turn left at traffic lights at 5.5km into Beach Road and Mouille Point. Pass Mouille Point lighthouse at 6km and turn into the Waterfront at 8km.

Set the stage

If you're still up for entertainment, it's showtime at theatres all around town. Check the press to see what's showing.

Cape Town's two main multi-venue theatres are Artscape (Foreshore, city centre) and the Baxter (Rondebosch), where'll you find everything from mainstream theatre to live music, dance, comedy and musicals, with Artscape also home to ballet and opera.

For work from local and international playwrights, go to the Theatre on the Bay (Camps Bay), the Intimate Theatre and the Little Theatre (both UCT Orange Street Campus).

For considerably more irreverence, visit On Broadway (Green Point and Table View), for a changing mix of comedy, drag and cabaret, or follow the Cape Comedy Collective stand-up comics at various venues around town. The Independent Armchair Theatre reflects Observatory's buzz, with live music, theatre, comedy and the odd film.

Kalk Bay Theatre regularly hosts famous South African names between a delicious dinner and dessert.

When the weather's good, watch Shakespeare under the stars at Maynardville Open-air Theatre (Wynberg, in January and February), or go further afield to more open-air amphitheatres at Oude Libertas (December to March) and Spier (November to March) near Stellenbosch.

And if you're looking for music to lift the soul, the Cape Town Philharmonic Orchestra moves around town between Artscape, the City Hall, St George's Cathedral and occasionally Kirstenbosch, where they often perform at New Year.

A bird's-eye view of Clifton

ABSEIL AFRICA (off Table Mountain) 021 424 4760, www.abseilafrica.com

BOULDERS PENGUINS 021 786 2329, www.cpnp.co.za, open daily 8:00–18:30

CAPE CARE ROUTE various operators: contact Cape Town Tourism, 021 426 4260

CAPE OF GOOD HOPE (Cape Point) 021 780 9200, www.cpnp.co.za, daily Oct–Mar 6:00–18:00 (exit 19:00), Apr–Sept 7:00–17:00 (exit 18:00), funicular runs from 9:00 to close

CAPE POINT OSTRICH FARM 021 780 9294, daily 9:30–17:30

CAPE TOWN TOURISM cnr Burg & Castle streets, 021 426 4260, www.cape-town.org

IMHOFF FARM Kommetjie, 021 783 4545, Tues–Sun 10:00–17:00

IMIZAMO YETHU TOWNSHIP TOURS 021 790 5827

KIRSTENBOSCH NATIONAL BOTANICAL GARDEN Rhodes Drive, 021 799 8800, www.nbi.ac.za, daily winter 8:00–18:00, summer 8:00–19:00

ROBBEN ISLAND MUSEUM 021 413 4200, www.robben-island.org.za

SOLELE GAME RESERVE Kommetjie, 021 785 3248

TABLE MOUNTAIN CABLEWAY 021 424 8181, www.tablemountain.net, opening times vary with season, but generally first car up at 8:30 (8:00 in Dec/Jan), last car down 19:00 or 20:00 (22:00 in Dec/Jan)

TOWNSHIP MUSIC TOURS (AND OTHER TOWNSHIP TOURS) various operators: call Cape Town Tourism, 021 426 4260

WORLD OF BIRDS Hout Bay, 021 790 2730, daily 9:00–17:00

SET THE STAGE

ARTSCAPE 021 421 7695 (dail-a-seat)

CAPE COMEDY COLLECTIVE 021 789 1665, www.samp.co.za

CAPE TOWN PHILHARMONIC ORCHESTRA 021 410 9809

VITAL INFO

INDEPENDENT ARMCHAIR THEATRE 021 447 1514

KALK BAY THEATRE 073 220 5430

LITTLE THEATRE AND INTIMATE THEATRE 021 480 7129

MAYNARDVILLE 021 421 7695 (Dial-a-seat)

ON BROADWAY 021 418 8338

OUDE LIBERTAS AMPHITHEATRE 021 809 7380

SPIER OPEN-AIR AMPHITHEATRE 021 809 1177

THEATRE ON THE BAY 021 438 3301

RESTAURANTS

AFRICA CAFÉ City Centre, 021 422 0221, dinners only

BERTHA'S RESTAURANT Simon's Town, 021 786 2138, daily, all meals

CAMEL ROCK RESTAURANT Scarborough, 021 780 1122, daily except Tues from 11:00

COBBS AT THE CAPE RESTAURANT Scarborough, 021 780 1480, daily, all meals

OLYMPIA CAFÉ Main Road, Kalk Bay, 021 788 6396, daily, all meals

TWO OCEANS RESTAURANT Cape Point, 021 780 9200, daily 9:30–17:30

CONSTANTIA WINE ROUTE

BUITENVERWACHTING 021 794 5190/1, closed Sun

CONSTANTIA UITSIG 021 794 1810, open daily, closed Mon lunch

CONSTANTIA WINE ROUTE 021 794 5128

GROOT CONSTANTIA 021 794 5128, open daily

KLEIN CONSTANTIA 021 794 5188, closed Sun

STEENBERG 021 713 2211, closed Sun

The unfinished flyover on Cape Town's foreshore is one of the city's more bizarre landmarks

Autumn turns the Cape's vineyards into a riot of rusty reds

THE ROUTE:

An intoxicating meander through a fine selection of award-winning wine estates, from hi-tech to homely and obvious to obscure in Stellenbosch and Franschhoek.

see MAP A

contact details on p 53

TIME: The route can be done as two separate days, or rolled together into one trip.

DISTANCE: About 200km or as separate day trips: Day One 170km, Day Two 140km.

BEST TIME TO GO: All year – warm summer days are perfect for chilled chardonnay under a shady oak, while winter delivers a completely different experience: many tasting areas have roaring fires. Cellar tours are more interesting in harvest time, during February and March, while autumn turns the vineyards to gold.

wine

INTRODUCTION

'Wine gives great pleasure; and every pleasure is of itself a good,' said Samuel Johnson. Well, we'll drink to that. Because you don't need to be a wine connoisseur to see the pleasure of spending a day (or two) meandering around the Cape Winelands, sampling wines that are among the finest in the world. What is tricky is choosing where to go, given that there are well over 100 wine estates in the Stellenbosch and Franschhoek areas alone.

To narrow the field a range of experts were gathered, including tourism officers, wine industry leaders and wine writers, and given a cruel task: to pick just a few of their favourites. The list was long, but some names came up again and again. So here they are, a selection of wine estates from hi-tech to historic, from huge to homely, that mix some of the grandes dames for first-timers with one or two little-known boutique estates for those who've done it all before. And they're kid-friendly too.

BEFORE YOU GO

- ✓ Sundays aren't good to tour the winelands, as most estates close for the weekend at lunchtime on Saturday. Of the estates listed here, only Spier in Stellenbosch and Chamonix and Môreson in Franschhoek are open on Sundays, with Boschendal joining them between November and April.

- ✓ Take some cash, as most estates charge a nominal fee for the tastings.

- ✓ Cellar tours must be booked a day or two in advance.

- ✓ Although there are presentations/tastings at Cabrière all week, those with Achim von Arnim are on Saturdays at 11:00 only.

Cape Dutch gables
adorn the farmhouses
of the winelands

The Cape's award-winning
wines have received
international acclaim for
more than a century

THE ROUTE

Spend Day One in Stellenbosch, South Africa's most famous wine region, then cross the Helshoogte Pass to Franschhoek, the 'French corner' that the Huguenot vignerons made their home.

Day One

- Wine tastings at Annandale, Waterford and Dornier
- Lunch at Spier
- More tastings at Middelvlei and Rustenberg
- Cross the Helshoogte Pass and overnight in Franschhoek

Day Two

- Visit Stony Brook and taste the wine
- Tour Cabrière with Achim von Arnim
- Lunch (and wine) at Môreson or Chamonix
- Afternoon tea at Boschendal

 FIND OUT MORE

- John Platter's *South African Wines* guide is a vital companion that lists the estates and grades the wines using a star system. It's updated each year.

- ✓ The Wine Desk at the Waterfront, in the Cape Town Tourism office in the Clock Tower Precinct, is a brilliant source of information, and they can book tours, arrange accommodation and help you ship wine home.

- ✓ For a 'gastronomic meander through the winelands', read *Cape Flavour* by Myrna Robins (Struik). This inventive book combines recipes with an overview of all the Cape wine routes and the fine food you'll find there, so you can recreate the experience at home.

- ✓ The *Winelands Good Time Guide* by Jean-Pierre Rossouw (Struik) gives a refreshingly different take on various wine estates and their characters.

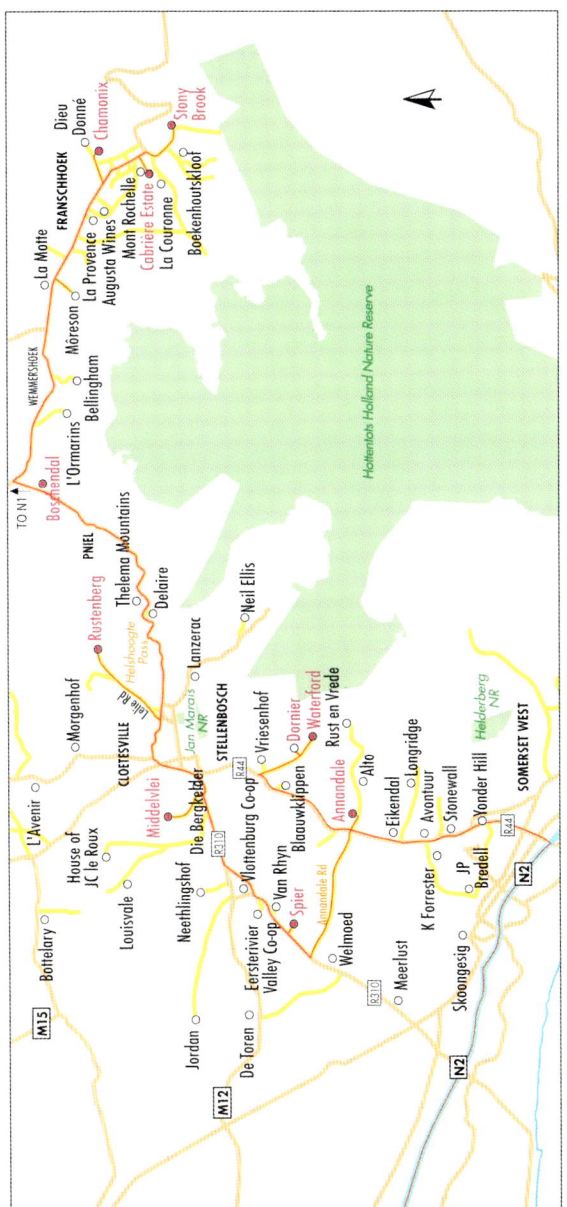

Tradition holds sway at Waterford, where real cork is still used

ONE

Waterfront to Annandale, Waterford and Dornier – 35min

From the Waterfront turn left to N1 Paarl, then follow N2 Somerset West signs. At about 43km, take Exit 43 Broadway Boulevard, Somerset West, and turn left to R44 Stellenbosch at the stop. At about 52km, turn right into Annandale Road (right after a farmstall with loads of scarecrows). Turn left into Annandale after 400m – signed Klein Akkerdraai and a small sign for Annandale. For Waterford and Dornier, turn right back onto the R44 to Stellenbosch. After 4.5km, turn right into Blaauwklippen Road (not the estate). Road becomes gravel.

If there's no-one about when you drive into Annandale, just do what the sign says and ring the old slave bell – you'll probably be met by a barefoot and smiling Hempies du Toit, or one of the family, surrounded by a jumble of dogs. A former Springbok rugby player (how many winemakers can explain the off-side rule so that anyone can understand it?), Hempies spent 25 years as winemaker at Alto, but now he is doing it for himself at Annandale, which is his own farm and also happens to be the oldest in the valley.

Among his best players are a cabernet sauvignon and an outstanding shiraz, created with all his own grapes in a 'low-tech and primitive cellar. But that's the way I like doing things, all hands-on'.

Personal and delightfully informal tastings (with swallows nesting in the beams overhead) happen in the ancient cellar – the farm's title deeds go back to 1688 – which, like the wine, is being left to age gracefully. I reckon the cobwebs hanging from the yellowwood ceiling in the barrel room are all original too! And for the rugby fans: if you ask, Hempies will sign your bottles.

It's hard to imagine a greater contrast at Dornier, which some may remember as Stellenrust, home to the original La Masseria Restaurant. Now owned by Swiss artist Christoph Dornier (yes, of the aircraft family), the estate has been remodelled along clean, stark lines, with an undulating silver roof designed by Dornier himself 'to enhance the landscape'.

The modern cellar and tasting area has a distinctly hi-tech, industrial feel, all raw brick, concrete and steel, with huge windows letting in natural light and the spectacular view of the Stellenberg Mountains. You don't need a cellar tour – more large windows allow you to look in on the enormous steel tanks. As a very special request, ask to see the barrel room, built beneath the large square dam. The Dornier estate encompasses three farms, and all Dornier's wines are blends, created thanks to their access to vineyards on different slopes.

And now for something completely different, again. A few kilometres further is Waterford, a fairly new winery created by well-known winemaker Kevin Arnold and the Ord family (who put the 'ord' in Waterford). The citrus orchard followed by a bank of lavender should give you a clue: Waterford is a little Italy, a winery built of dry stone walls around a square with the trademark fountain in the middle.

Geese serve a dual purpose as watchdogs and snail hunters

Terracotta pots, pale green shutters, a game of boules in progress, good wine and cushions on the wall around the fountain invite you to kick off your shoes and embrace *la dolce vita*. The U-shaped winery flows around the square – the cellar tour takes you from the bottling and labelling machinery in one wing, past the tanks to the barrel room dimly lit by chandeliers in the other. And if it's chilly, settle into one of the deep couches and enjoy tastings in front of the roaring fire.

R44 to Spier – 10min

From Waterford and Dornier, turn left onto the R44 heading back to Somerset West. After about 4.5km, turn right into Annandale Road. At the T-junction turn right on R310 Stellenbosch. Spier is on the right after 1.5km.

Spier is firmly entrenched on the tour bus circuit, but it's an important stop simply because it's grown far beyond a historic wine estate into a destination that can keep you entertained for an entire weekend. (And it's big enough for you to find your own quiet space under the trees on the banks of the Eerste River, away from the madding crowds.)

Before the wine gets overlooked in all the activities on offer, head for the Wine Centre, an original Dutch gabled barn dating to 1750, where over 220 local and 10 international wine estates are showcased. Spier holds tastings of various local wines, not just their own – seven wines are selected for tastings on the hour,

of which two will be Spier or one of its labels (Longridge, Bay View, Capelands, Savanah, Sejana and Naledi). The Spier Private Collection is the premium range, made from grapes hand selected from single, mature low-yield vineyards, with limited quantities released each year. Not surprisingly they shine with stars in the Platter guide.

Then, lunch: choose from a create-your-own (but not 'bring your own'!) picnic around the dam or at the river, a riverside pub and grill, or the Jonkershuis offering a traditional Cape Malay buffet. But you'll probably be seduced by Moyo (which means soul in Swahili), a fabulous barbecue experience which sprawls through the gardens, up onto platforms in the trees and into gorgeous Bedouin-style tents with decadently comfortable loungers on the lawn. The décor, a fantasy of North Africa meets Cape Africa, will delight you – Moroccan-style lanterns hang from the trees above wine barrels stained in the rich ochres and purples of the Bo-Kaap. Even the waiters, serving Pan-African cuisine, are decorated! This is even more impressive at night, when light comes from only the moon and flickering lanterns.

If you can drag yourself away, after lunch visit the cheetah outreach programme and the raptor rehab centre for injured or confiscated birds, or take your pick from a museum of African art in the original manor house, weavers, jewellers, golf, tennis and horse riding, with a special programme to entertain the kids (see Kids Route p 116 for more). Enjoy the Spier Summer Arts festival at night from December to March, which celebrates everything from opera to theatre and pop.

Spier to Middelvlei – 15min

Turn right out of Spier. At about 3.5km turn right at T-junction onto R310 Stellenbosch. At 6.5km (opposite Distell) turn left into Oude Libertas Road and left into Middelvlei.

Although you drive through a suburb to get there, the Middelvlei gates deliver you right into the middle of the perfect country farmyard, complete with a charming manor house, roses and green lawns, old barns, woolly donkeys in a meadow, ducks, geese, turkeys and goats with a couple of wallabies thrown in. The kids can go wild in this welcoming atmosphere while you sip

Don't let it go to your head...

Make sure you include a non-drinker or someone prepared to spit in your party to do the driving. The legal limit is 0,05g alcohol per 100ml blood, which in real terms means that after one to two glasses of wine you can't get behind the wheel. (Your body can process about one glass per hour.)

wines made by the Mombergs (the fourth generation is waiting in the wings to continue the family farm tradition), with happy photos of the family decorating the walls of the tasting room, a converted stable. Children can also visit aviaries where Ben Momberg breeds parrots, rather appropriately on a farm at the foot of the Papegaaiberg ('Parrot Mountain'), or chat to the talking crow. Ask about Stiljan ('Quiet Jan') and his cousin Janbek ('Mouthy Jan') whom South Africans will remember as politician and athlete Jannie Momberg. Middelvlei Pinotage is the flagship red among merlot and cabernet sauvignon, but do try the divine, lightly wooded chardonnay. It is possible to tour the traditional cellar by appointment during harvest season.

Middelvlei to Rustenberg – 13min

Leave Middelvlei and turn left at the T-junction onto the R310. Enter Stellenbosch and stay left after you cross Dorp Street.

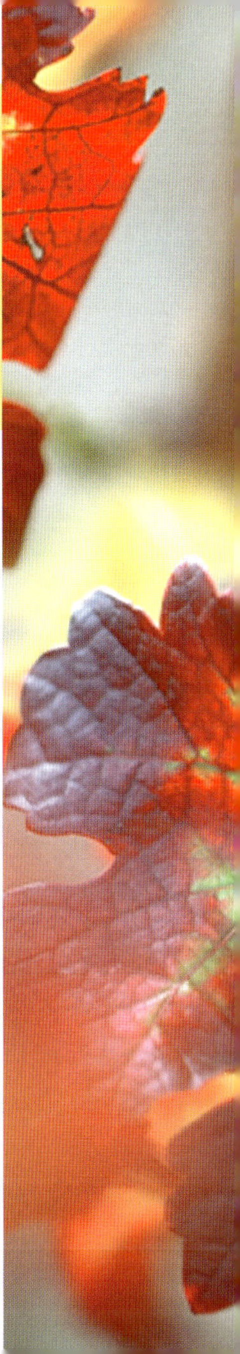

The Huguenot Monument in Franschhoek

THE FRENCH HUGUENOTS

The Edict of Nantes, which granted tolerance of the Protestant religion, was revoked by Louis XIV in 1685. This led to large-scale emigration of Huguenots to the colonies, including the Cape, to start a new life – and bolster the fledgling wine industry. So many settled in Oliphantshoek, named for the elephants who calved here, that the area came to be called Le Quartier Français and later Franschhoek (French Corner).

Cross Bird Street at the traffic lights, following N1 Paarl, then turn right at next lights to R310 Franschhoek, Helshoogte Road (about 4.5km). Turn left into Lelie Road. Rustenberg is on the left at about 8.5km.

Leave Stellenbosch behind on the drive that winds between vineyards, orchards and paddocks to reach Rustenberg, and you're transported into a picture of what the region must have looked like 100 years ago. Rustenberg is, quite simply, breathtakingly beautiful. From the historic gabled manor house, where even the brick steps are worn from hundreds of years of footsteps, you can see very little other than vineyards, tall green trees and cultivated fields stretching all the way to the

Simonsberg mountains rising majestically above the estate. By contrast, owner Simon Barlow embraces the latest technology in winemaking, with a broad range of multi-award-winning wines (Rustenberg and Brampton labels) tasted in a gracious yet modern tasting room, which used to be the old horse stables. The estate recently won an award for architecture, as an excellent example of avant-garde meets historic. Spend time in the beautiful formal gardens created by Rozanne Barlow, Simon's wife, and walk the soul-inspiring labyrinth, which follows the design found in the Chartres Cathedral in France.

Rustenberg to Franschhoek
via Helshoogte Pass – 13min

Drive back down Lelie Road to the stop. Turn left onto Helshoogte Road and follow signs for Franschhoek through Pniel and past Boschendal. At T-junction turn right onto the R45 Franschhoek. Enter Franschhoek at 28km; the tourism bureau is on the right at 30km. End the day in Franschhoek so you can make an early start in the morning, with the wine estates right on your doorstep. There are several guesthouses in Franschhoek itself, and even more on the surrounding farms – see Where to Stay on p 53 or ask the tourism bureau for more details.

Franschhoek Tourism to Stony Brook – 6min

Continue up Franschhoek's main road, Huguenot Street, then turn right at the T-junction at the Huguenot Monument. At about 3km, turn left to Stony Brook.

You'll feel like you're dropping in on a friend for tea at Stony Brook, a family-run estate near the top of the Franschhoek valley. Settle down for a chat and a laugh with Joy McNaught who'll give you lots of personal attention while you taste the wine on the terrace of the family home (or indoors in front of a fire in winter). You may or may not see her husband Nigel, who prefers to make the wine 'unless I wrestle him out here by the ear!' says Joy. This is an intimate estate, well off the beaten tourist track, run by a couple who make every effort to be as 'green' as possible. They're officially closed in the afternoons, but phone ahead or take your chances – aside from having to nip off to collect a child from school, Joy will almost certainly open for you. They export more than 60 percent of their wine, which gets plenty of stars in the Platter wine guide.

Stony Brook to Cabrière – 5min

Retrace your route to the Monument, and turn left down Huguenot Street. Take first left into Berg Street, and follow it to Cabrière Estate.

We're back in tourist country at Cabrière Estate, but even though the groups can be big, flamboyant, sabre-wielding wine grower Achim von Arnim creates a personal touch when he takes the

cellar tours on Saturday mornings. Guests enjoy the tours only marginally more than this Prussian aristocrat does himself, and his off-beat humour, enthusiasm and clear delight in life are infectious. Although the range includes still wines and a fortified chardonnay apéritif, the star of the show, aside from Achim, is the Méthode Cap Classique sparkling wine, bottle fermented in the traditional Champagne style. The cellar tour takes you through the fascinating fermentation and turning process (with plenty of anecdotes to make you giggle), before the tasting and sabrage, where, with dramatic flair, Achim opens the bottles with a shining silver sabre.

Achim's tours last till about 13:00 (the weekday tastings are shorter), so you're probably ready for lunch. Stroll to Haute Cabrière Cellar Restaurant, or combine lunch with another tasting at Cape Chamonix or Môreson.

Cabrière to Chamonix and Môreson – 5 and 7min

Return up Berg Street and turn left into Huguenot Street. Pass the tourism bureau, then turn right into Uitkyk Street to Chamonix or continue for another 4.5km and turn left onto the Happy Valley Road to Môreson.

Enjoy casual French cuisine (what else?) at Chamonix, where you can eat in the gabled homestead or outside under shady trees with magnificent views over the valley. Or order a picnic and eat on the lawn – plenty of space for the kids to explore (there's also a children's menu and jungle gym). Then cross the

The textures and colours of the ever-changing vines

EATING OUT IN FRANSCHHOEK

At the risk of angering the entire national restaurant fraternity, let us say: prepare to dine in the gourmet capital of South Africa. Franschhoek's restaurants frequently appear among the top 10 in the country, with gastronomic heights regularly reached by Le Quartier Français (voted among top 50 in the world), Bijoux, Monneaux, Haute Cabrière Cellar Restaurant among many more. Indulge – you won't be disappointed at all. Or simply stroll along Huguenot Road, the town's main street, and take your pick from restaurants that spill out onto the pavement. (Look out for the fromagerie and a Belgian chocolatier.)

road to the tasting centre, housed in the quaint old blacksmith's cottage, with an underground tunnel leading down into the cellar (tours by appointment). The emphasis is on fine wines (Chamonix was the only South African gold medallist at the International Chardonnay du Monde 2000 competition in France), but for a distinct change of pace, try the German-style schnapps, Swedish bitters and grappa. And if you're now in no state to drive home, spend the night in one of their chalets or at the luxurious hunting lodge on the hill (but be prepared to be watched by various hunted, now seriously stuffed, animals on the wall).

The best time to visit Môreson is in February for the annual Blessing of the Harvest festival. Fill your basket with grapes from the vineyard, extract the juice (that is, get your shoes off, jump in the barrel and start stomping), then enjoy lunch while you design your own label. A few months later, 'your' wine will be available for collection! Another fine way the folk at Môreson make it impossible to leave is to offer courses in the art of bread-making at Bread & Wine, the rustic, Mediterranean-style restaurant on the farm – you'll want to copy their heavenly, crusty home-baked breads served inside or in the courtyard. The tasting room is next door, where you can sample award-winning wines under the Môreson ('morning sun') and Pinehurst labels.

Tours by appointment.

Lavender lends a Continental touch

Franschhoek to Cape Town – 1hr

From the Môreson/Happy Valley Road turn left onto the main road out of Franschhoek. For Boschendal, turn left at 9.4km to R310 Stellenbosch. The estate is 1.5km further. Otherwise continue straight, then turn left to Klapmuts at 13km. At about 22km, T-junction right on R44 Wellington. At about 23km turn left onto N1 Cape Town. Stay on the N1 into the city, and follow signs for the Waterfront.

Stop for afternoon tea at Boschendal to see what everyone's been talking about for years. Arguably the most gracious of the wine estates, Boschendal has turned tourism into a major business, but retains its stature as one of the most elegant of them all. Wines covering all bases – reds, whites and sparkling, which twinkle with stars in the Platter wine guide – can be tasted at the Taphuis, before an hour-long walk through the vineyards to a spectacular viewpoint on the slopes of the Simonsberg (book in advance).

Have tea and scones at Le Café, in the old slave quarters of Boschendal Manor House (now a museum). Boschendal is also famous for Le Pique-Nique, with hampers served from a gazebo on the lawn, or go for the full Cape cuisine buffet lunch at the restaurant in the original cellar.

STILL THIRSTY?

See the Country Route, pp 68–81, for more wine estates in Robertson, and the Cheese Route, pp 54–67, for tastings around Paarl and Wellington. Wines of the Hemel-en-Aarde Valley feature in the Whale Route, p 183.

STELLENBOSCH

ANNANDALE 021 881 3560/1, Mon–Fri 10:00–17:00, Sat 10:00–16:00

DORNIER 021 880 0557, Mon–Fri 9:00–16:30, Sat 10:00–15:00

MIDDELVLEI 021 883 2565, Mon–Sat 10:00–16:30

RUSTENBERG 021 809 1200, Mon–Fri 9:00–17:00, Sat 10:00–13:30

SPIER 021 809 1100, tastings daily 9:00–17:00

WATERFORD 021 880 0496, Mon–Fri 8:00–17:00, Sat 10:00–13:00

FRANSCHHOEK

BOSCHENDAL 021 870 4200, Mon–Sat 8:30–16:30 (Nov–Apr Sun 9:30–12:30)

CABRIÉRE ESTATE 021 876 2630, Sat tastings and tours with Achim von Arnim at 11:00, Mon–Fri tastings with Hildegard von Arnim and colleagues at 11:00 and 15:00, sales Mon–Fri 9:00–17:00, Sat 10:00–14:00

CAPE CHAMONIX 021 876 2494, daily 9:00–16:30, Chamonix Restaurant 021 876 2393, daily 12:00–16:00, dinner on Fri

MÔRESON 021 876 3055, daily 11:00–17:00, Bread & Wine Restaurant 021 876 3692, Wed–Sun 12:00–16:00

STONY BROOK 021 876 2182, Mon–Sat 9:00–13:00

WINE ROUTE INFORMATION

FRANSCHHOEK WINE VALLEY & TOURISM ASSOCIATION 021 876 3603

STELLENBOSCH WINE ROUTE 021 886 4310

WINE DESK AT THE WATERFRONT 021 405 4550

WHERE TO STAY:

BLUEBERRY HILL 021 876 3362

KLEIN DASSENBERG 021 876 2107

KLEIN OLIPHANTSHOEK 021 876 2566

LA VERDURE 021 876 3239

LE MANOIR DE BRENDEL 021 876 3715

LE QUARTIER FRANCAIS (RELAIS & CHATEAU) 021 876 3016

The goat tower at Fairview

THE ROUTE:
Nibble your way through camembert and caseggio around Paarl and Wellington, with the occasional olive and glass of wine, of course.

see MAP A

contact details on p 67

TIME: One (full) day

DISTANCE: About 180km

BEST TIME TO GO: Any time, although April to June is most interesting for olives, as that is when they're being harvested and processed.

cheese & olives

INTRODUCTION

The happy marriage between wine and cheese is nowhere more apparent than in the Cape Winelands, with olives and olive oils completing the picture: imagine a long table in the dappled shade of a vineyard terrace, with good friends sharing laughter and simple food as the shadows lengthen towards evening. In the mood?

Then slow down and swap the city for a valley where nature sets the pace, where deadlines are measured in seasons not minutes, where handcrafted cheeses and oils are left to mature in their own good time.

The people you'll meet are as warm as the sun on your back as you meander through the beautifully scenic greater Paarl area, before moving on to Wellington, settled by the French Huguenots in 1688.

READING LIST

- ✓ *Olives and oils in South Africa*, by Wendy Flanagan and Reni Hildenbrand (Mbira Press), is probably the definitive word on the South African industry – aside from general info on olives, it showcases and rates all the local producers. (You can buy a copy from Reni on the estate, see p 63.)

- ✓ If you love good food (and jaunts into the country to see where it comes from), get *Eat In* magazine, available in bookstores, which lists more yummy food shops, delis and interesting farms than you could visit in a lifetime.

- ✓ In the same vein, Cape Town's Giggling Gourmet, aka Jenny Morris, is in touch with the boutique producers of fine food. Visit her website for the latest foodie news at www.gigglinggourmet.com

Stuffed olives

Creamy Brie cheese

THE ROUTE

- Taste the cheese at Anura
- Detour to Fairview
- Catch up on what you missed at Cotage Fromage
- Pop into Paarl's wicked chocolate delicatessen
- Lunch at Hildenbrand Wine and Olive Estate
- Taste the wine at Bovlei
- Another wine tasting at Rhebokskloof
- Dinner (and more cheese) at La Masseria

BEFORE YOU GO

✓ Have a hearty breakfast – you'll be tempted to taste wine at all these estates along with all the delicious cheeses and olives.

✓ Sundays are rest days in the country – only Anura, Cotage Fromage, Hildenbrand and Rhebokskloof remain open, the rest all close for the day.

✓ La Masseria is closed on Mondays and Sunday nights.

✓ Hildenbrand Wine and Olive Estate is open for tastings daily, but the restaurant is closed on Tuesdays (have lunch at Cotage Fromage or Oude Wellington, a few kilometres past Bovlei, instead).

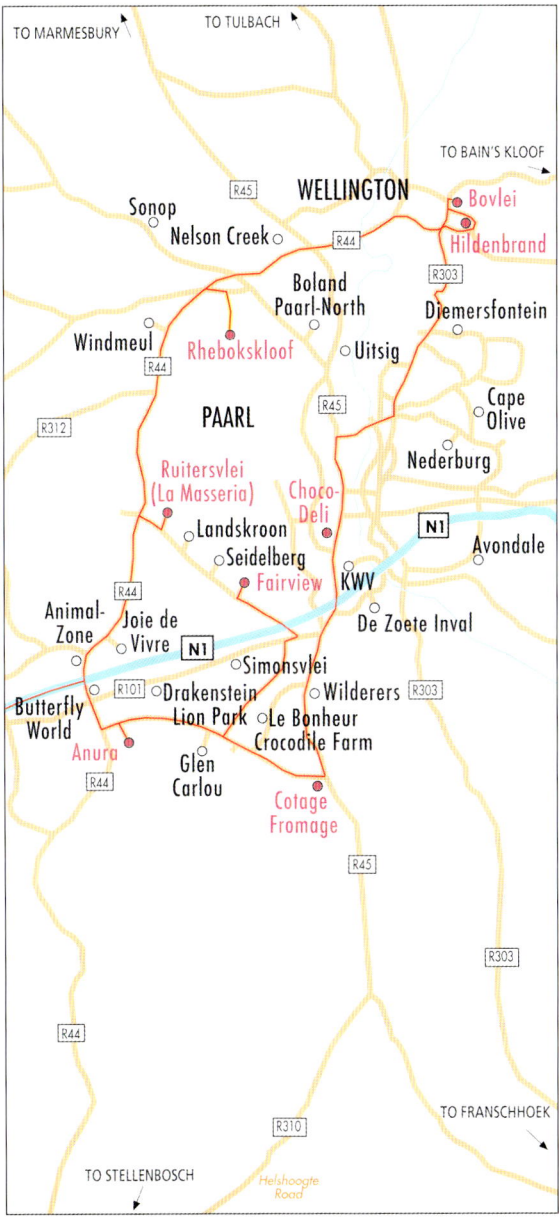

TO MARMESBURY

TO TULBACH

TO BAIN'S KLOOF

R45

WELLINGTON

Sonop

Nelson Creek

R44

Bovlei

Hildenbrand

R303

Boland
Paarl-North

Diemersfontein

Windmeul

R44

Rhebokskloof

Uitsig

Cape
Olive

R312

PAARL

R45

Nederburg

Ruitersvlei
(La Masseria)

Choco-
Deli

N1

Avondale

Landskroon

Seidelberg

Fairview

KWV

R44

Animal-
Zone

Joie de
Vivre

De Zoete Inval

N1

Simonsvlei

Butterfly
World

R101

Drakenstein
Lion Park

Wilderers

R303

Le Bonheur
Crocodile Farm

Anura

R44

Glen
Carlou

Cotage
Fromage

R45

R303

R44

TO FRANSCHHOEK

R310

TO STELLENBOSCH

Helshoogte
Road

The tasting room at Anura

Waterfront to Anura – 30min

From the Waterfront turn left onto the highway and keep following signs for N1 Paarl. At about 45km take Exit 47, R44 Stellenbosch, Klapmuts, and turn right at the stop. At 46.6km, turn left to R45 Franschhoek. Anura is 600m along this road.

Ponds full of platannas (a type of frog) greet you at Anura, which is Latin for frog, and when it rains the sound is deafening. They welcome you into a lovely tasting room with long oak tables overlooking the barrel room and green lawns. Get comfortable, as there are plenty of cheeses to taste. The Forest Hill Cheesery at Anura specialises in white mould cheeses – brie and camembert – using Jersey milk from Rustenberg (see the Wine Route pp 45–47) and Ayrshire milk from Glen Carlou. Their traditional

AYRSHIRE OR JERSEY?

Milk from Jersey cows is traditionally used to make a variety of cheeses. Ayrshire milk has a slightly lower butterfat and protein content, with a 'softer' fat that makes it more digestible and better for cooking.

camembert and brie have both won 'Best in South Africa' awards at the National Cheese Festival, but make space for their flavoured bries, with green figs, green peppercorns, chives or apricots soaked in port. All are made using non-animal rennet.

Detour to Fairview – 8min

Turn right out of Anura. Then left onto the Simonsvlei Road, which is gravel. At about 4.8km, T-junction right onto the R101 (tar). At 5.4km, turn left onto the Suid-Agter Paarl Road, signed to Seidelberg, Ruitersvlei. Cross the highway. Fairview is on the right at 7.7km.

While frogs rule Anura, goats are king at Fairview. You'll park beneath their snooty stares from the trademark goat tower, before going inside to taste a huge range of award-winning cheeses made from both goats' and cows' milk, alongside even more award-winning wines – owner Charles Back was recently voted South Africa's wine person of the decade. And you have to laugh at their 'Goats do Roam' wine label that had the French makers of Côte du Rhône wine all in a tizz. Their La Beryl won best Pont l'Evéque and the Roydon best camembert at the 2003 World Cheese Awards, so be sure to taste those along with plenty of chevins, white moulds and blue cheeses and even a 'white' blue without the blue vein. They're all available in a comprehensive cheese shop that also sells tasting platters of seven styles if you can't make up your mind. The kids will enjoy watching the goats being milked, and if you visit in July and August, there'll be plenty of kids (of the baby goat kind) to keep you enchanted. As you leave Fairview, stop for a moment at the opposite field for a glimpse of zebra, bontebok and eland.

Fairview to Cotage Fromage – 14min

Turn left out of Fairview. At the T-junction turn right on to the R101, Kraaifontein. After 600m turn left onto Simonsvlei Road and left again at the T-junction onto tar. At 11.5km turn into Vrede en Lust.

If you're the kind of person who likes good food to come to you, rather than driving halfway round the countryside to find it, you'll be in heaven at Cotage Fromage, a decadent deli and restaurant on the Vrede en Lust estate. Aside from a smorgasbord of between 50 and 60 local cheeses, along with the pick of olives and olive oils, you'll battle to leave without stocking up on other delicious goodies that go with cheese, like chilli jams, pestos, pickled brinjals, orange roll and fig preserves. Cotage Fromage also gives you the opportunity to taste cheese and olive oils from estates that are either far off this route or aren't generally open

DID YOU KNOW?

There's no difference between brie and camembert, other than their shape and size? Brie, made in rounds up to 1kg, and camembert, in rounds from 60g–250g, taste different because of the surface area of mould, which matures the cheese. Camembert is stronger, simply because the ratio of mould to cheese is greater than brie. (Brie is cut into triangles purely for retail purposes.)

Cheese and olives complement each other

to the public, like delicious Dalewood Fromage or Vesuvio and Maradadi oils. The restaurant serves light meals (how about crumbed, deep-fried gorgonzola in a berry and biltong sauce?) in a lovely outdoor area with a jungle gym for the kids.

Cotage Fromage to Paarl – 20min

Cross railway line, at T-junction turn left onto the R45 Paarl. At 6km, T-junction right onto R101 Paarl. Choco-Deli is on the left at 10km.

Look out for De Oude Paarl boutique hotel in Paarl's main street, for there you'll find Choco-Deli, a wickedly delicious emporium devoted entirely to fine Belgian chocolate.

There are fresh deliveries every Wednesday, although the chocs have a perfectly respectable shelf life (but they are not likely to last that long at all).

Paarl to Hildenbrand – 20min

Continue along the main street as it doglegs right then left. At traffic lights (about 13.5km) turn right into Optenhorst Road to Wellington, Paarl East. Cross two bridges, at next lights turn left onto R301. As road curves left into Wellington (about 23.5km) turn right into Blouvlei Road, signed for Klein Rhebokskloof. Turn into Hildenbrand Wine and Olive Estate at about 28.5km – it's easy to overshoot.

If ever you had a childhood fantasy of owning a farm when you grew up, it probably looked like Klein Rhebokskloof, home of Hildenbrand Wine and Olive Estate. A charmingly haphazard cluster of ancient Cape Dutch buildings set in beautiful gardens, it's patrolled by five dogs, nine cats, some fearsome blue-eyed

geese and a motley collection of farm animals and foundlings nurtured by owner, oil- and winemaker Reni Hildenbrand. Klein Rhebokskloof is the birthplace of the South African olive industry as the country's first orchard for production was planted on this farm in 1893. Reni, after learning her skills in Tuscany, is now continuing the tradition, producing top quality cold-pressed extra virgin and the deeply desirable unpressed extra virgin olive oil, caught before the actual pressing process has begun. (Be quick though, as demand is outstripping production.) You can also taste table olives and an award-winning range of red and white wines. Enjoy lunch on the terrace while the kids explore the farmyard. Look out for Emma, the goat who thinks she's a sheep when she's not being a dog, whose best friend is Patty Yolanda, the pig. And ask why the tiny pony, acquired as a friend for the ox, is called Try Me. Spend the night in the guesthouse if you've had too much wine. Phone ahead if you want to tour the cellar and olive room.

Hildenbrand to La Masseria, via Bovlei and Rhebokskloof – 35min, excluding stops

Turn left out of Hildenbrand. At 2.8km T-junction right on R301. Bovlei is on the right at 4.6km. From Boveli, retrace your route into Wellington. T-junction left at the church. At about 9km, turn right at the traffic lights R44 Kaapstad (Cape Town) into Champagne Street. At about 18km turn left into Rhebokskloof, or continue straight on to about 27km, turn left into Suid-Agter Paarl Road. Turn left to Ruitersvlei and La Masseria after 300m.

Where next? The route finishes with more cheese for dinner, but before that there's a chance to stock the home cellars at two wine estates offering great value-for-money wines.

Bovlei's cellar is right on the road, offering a good range of easy drinking, quality wines.

The sun should be starting to turn the vineyards golden by now, making the drive to La Masseria even more scenic. En route stop at Rhebokskloof for wines suiting all tastes and pockets The estate is set amid fruit orchards and vineyards and surrounded by fynbos. But be sure to get to La Masseria in time for sundowners before the party starts…

cheese & olives

When the moon hits your eye like a big pizza pie, you're most likely to be happily singing along at La Masseria, the family-run Italian restaurant that's now moved to

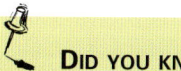
Ruitersvlei farm on the Suid-Agter Paarl Road – there's another one in Eversdal Cellars in Durbanville. Mother-and-daughter team Salomie and Delia Pacifico will make sure you fill up on a mouth-watering buffet of antipasto or home-made pastas from the menu, but do remember to save space for the cheese made by dad Donato at the cheese factory in Stellenbosch, which is also worth a visit, at Delvera Farm off the R44.

Actor Anthony Kampf (you'll recognise his face from stage and screen) is on the guitar and working magic between the tables, so by the end of the evening, after rousing choruses of 'That's Amore', 'Buona Sera' and 'Volare', the entire restaurant departs as new best friends.

Cheeses range from hard pecorino and monte, through feta to sweetmilk taleggio, pepper and chilli caseggios, award-winning mozzarella filone with heavenly dessert cheeses to finish. You must try the duetto dolce – mascarpone with preserved figs and walnuts. Be sure to book a table.

La Masseria to Waterfront – 35min

Turn right out of Ruitersvlei onto Suid-Agter Paarl Road. T-junction left R44 Stellenbosch. At 6.5km turn right to N1 Cape Town. Follow N1 into city, then follow Waterfront signs.

Still want more? These are either open-to-the-public operations that are off this route, or are working farms that are not really geared for visitors, but you can visit by appointment (give them a day or two's warning):

- Dalewood Fromage, for heavenly white mould cheeses
- Foxenburg Estate, for cheese, olives, olive oils and organically grown, fresh mushrooms.
- Wellmont, where you can view cheese being made.

- Cape Olive Trust, which sells the Buffet olive range.
- Drakenstein Olives, for your olives, olive oils and green tapenade.

Take the kids to...

- Butterfly World – you can walk through a cloud of butterflies in the largest tropical butterfly park in Africa. Take Exit 47 and turn right.
- Drakenstein Lion Farm – see the real thing in a sanctuary for rescued lions. Pass Butterfly World, then turn left and drive 5km.
- AnimalZone – all sorts of exotic and local creatures such as llamas, monkeys, ostriches, emus and snakes. Also farm animals including birds, rabbits and goats. Take Exit 47 and turn left.
- Le Bonheur crocodile farm – see crocs from hatchlings to retirement age. Look for signs off the R45.

TASTING OLIVE OIL

Most properly served in a shot glass, the oil is first sniffed for fruitiness (usually grassy, almonds, leaves, apples, green tomatoes or green bananas). It's then sipped and judged for the desirable bitter taste, before the pungent aftertaste, often described as peppery, is felt in the throat. In a quality oil, all three elements – fruitiness, bitterness and pungency – are well balanced.

ANURA WINE & CHEESE 021 875 5360, Mon–Fri 9:30–16:00, Sat–Sun 10:00–16:00, www.foresthillcheese.co.za

BOVLEI 021 873 1567, Mon–Fri 8:30–12:30, 13:30–17:00, Sat 8:30–12:30, www.bovlei.co.za

CHOCO-DELI De Oude Paarl Boutique Hotel, 32 Main Street, Paarl, 021 872 1002, Mon–Fri 9:00–18:00, Sat–Sun 10:00–17:00, www.deoudepaarl.com

COTAGE FROMAGE ON VREDE EN LUST 021 874 3991, daily 9:00–18:00, www.vnl.co.za

FAIRVIEW 021 863 2450, Mon–Fri 8:30–17:00, Sat 8:30–13:00, www.fairview.co.za

HILDENBRAND WINE & OLIVE ESTATE ON KLEIN RHEBOKSKLOOF off Blouvlei Road (the horseshoe road) Wellington, 021 873 4115, tastings daily 10:00–16:00, restaurant daily except Tues for lunches, open for dinner if there are bookings: 083 384 0249, www.wine-estate-hildenbrand.co.za

LA MASSERIA Ruitersvlei, off the Suid–Agter Paarl Road, 021 863 3637, open for all meals, closed Mon and Sun nights, www.lamasseria.co.za

RHEBOKSKLOOF 021 869 8386, daily 9:00–17:00, www.rhebokskloof.co.za

STILL WANT MORE?

CAPE OLIVE TRUST turn off the Swawelstert Road, Daljosafat, 021 868 3120

DALEWOOD FROMAGE off the Franschhoek Simondium Road, 021 875 5725

DRAKENSTEIN OLIVES De Hoop Farm, Swawelstert Road, Daljosafat, 021 868 3185

FOXENBURG ESTATE Agter Groenberg Farm, Wellington, 021 873 5617

WELLMONT Interlude Farm, Blouvlei, Wellington, 021 864 1181

PAARL VINTERS 021 872 3605, www.paarlwine.co.za

FOR THE KIDS

ANIMALZONE 021 875 5063, daily 9:00–17:00, www.animalzone.co.za

BUTTERFLY WORLD 021 875 5628, daily 9:00–17:00

DRAKENSTEIN LION FARM 021 863 3290, daily 9:30–17:00, feeding time Mon, Wed, Fri at 16:00

LE BONHEUR CROC FARM 021 863 1142, daily 9:00–17:00

TYGERBERG ZOO 021 884 4494, daily 9:00–17:00

REGIONAL TOURISM BUREAUS

PAARL TOURISM 021 872 3829, www.paarlonline.com

WELLINGTON TOURISM 021 873 4604, www.visitwellington.co.za

Cactus garden at Soekershof

THE ROUTE:
Kick off your shoes and relax as you explore the vine-clad countryside around Robertson, the 'valley of wine and roses'.
see MAP A
contact details on p 81

TIME: One day, although you may want to make it a weekend and include McGregor or Montagu. Better still would be a few days to take in the entire Route 62.

DISTANCE: About 380km as a round trip

BEST TIME TO GO: All year, although it's particularly beautiful in November and December when jacarandas, cannas and roses make the route a riot of colour. Grape harvest time is February and March, when there's lots of activity in the cellars, and autumn is charming too, when the vineyards slowly turn to rust and gold.

country

INTRODUCTION

All city-stressed souls need to flee to the country now and then, for champagne air and wholesome food in a calming green landscape to soothe jangled nerves. So here's a day designed around pure indulgence, for enjoying fine wines and good friends, with the sun on your back as the river glides lazily by. All in an area of back-to-back vineyards interrupted only by fruit orchards and stud farms, with magnificent thoroughbreds posing in lush meadows.

The other good thing about the Robertson valley, especially for those who've been there, done that, is that because it's placed almost precisely between the two main highways out of Cape Town, it's often overlooked as we speed along the N1 or N2. But while it's not on the way to anywhere, it might tempt you onto Route 62, the 'world's longest wine route' that stretches all the way past Montagu to Oudtshoorn and Uniondale. So go for the day – but know that you might be away from the city for a while.

READING LIST

- ✓ *Cape Flavour* by Myrna Robins (Struik) is a tribute to the Western Cape's 12 wine regions. Filled with regional recipes and specialities, this is a book that is sure to delight all lovers of food and wine.
- ✓ An excellent source of information on activities and accommodation in this area, and in particular Route 62, can be found at www.route62.co.za.

Traditional rural furnishings

Tranquil country afternoon

THE ROUTE

- Taste the wines of Graham Beck, Van Loveren and De Wetshof
- Sip Viljoensdrift wines aboard a boat drifting down the Breede River
- Have a picnic on the Breede or eat at Fraai Uitzicht 1798
- Get lost in the largest hedge maze in the world and explore the cactus garden at Soekershof, or be dazzled by the parrots at Birds of Paradise
- Head for the river again for sundowners and dinner aboard the Kolgans floating restaurant

BEFORE YOU GO

✓ The Viljoensdrift wine cruises take place on Saturdays and the first Sunday of the month (every Sunday in December). If you're visiting during the week, taste the wines in the cellar, then make the Kolgans trip a lunchtime cruise.

✓ Fraai Uitzicht 1798 is closed for meals on Mondays and Tuesdays (except for overnight guests).

✓ The Graham Beck, De Wetshof and Van Loveren wine estates are all closed on Sundays. Try Bon Cape Organic Wine instead.

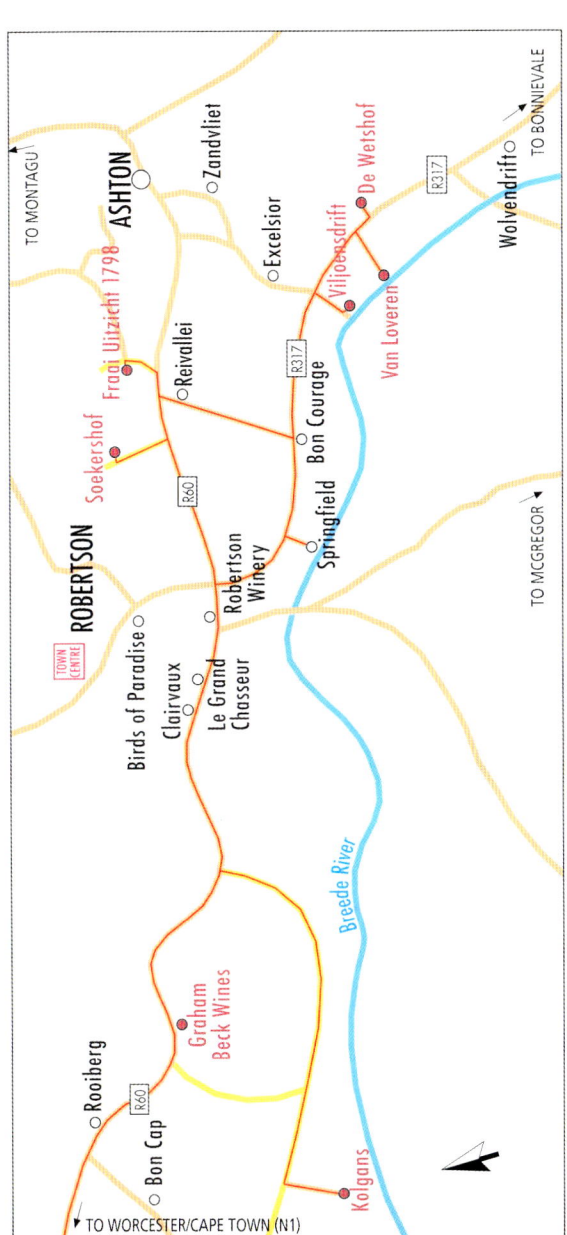

Waterfront to Graham Beck – 1hr 30min

From the Waterfront turn left onto highway following signs for N1 Paarl. At 61km follow signs for N1 Worcester and pay a toll fee to use the Huguenot Tunnel at 66km. Ignore the first turn into Worcester (signed R43 Villiersdorp). At the second set of traffic lights, about 107km, turn right to Worcester/Robertson. At 109km turn left at the lights onto R60 Robertson, and turn right at the next lights into Robertson Road, R60. Turn right into Graham Beck at about 147km. Graham Beck sparkles in the galaxy of South African wines, and a sip of these bubbles will get the day off to a suitably uplifting start. (They certainly worked for Nelson Mandela – the Graham Beck Brut was selected for his inauguration in 1994.)

Don't expect anything Cape Dutch: metal sculptures in the vineyard prepare you for fabulously avant garde architecture in purple, orange and green, which looks better than it sounds. The purple reflects the indigenous vygies, the green the fynbos and

Old meets new at Graham Beck

the orange the sand and soil of the Klein Karoo. The wines cover a wide range, but most famous of all are their magnificent Methode Cap Classique sparklers. Cellar tours by appointment only, phone and book.

Graham Beck to Robertson – 6min

Turn right out of Graham Beck onto R60 Robertson. Enter the town at 7km, the tourism office is on the corner of Voortrekker and Reitz streets at about 8km.

Robertson is a charming Boland town, with lovely examples of Victorian and Georgian homes – drive up Paul Kruger and Van Reenen streets to have a look. But that's not why you're here.

So after a quick look at the town, head straight out on the Bonnievale road to the riverside wine estates, starting at De Wetshof and working your way back. Watch your time as the river cruise starts at 11:00 or 12:00. Do phone ahead.

More to do in Robertson: Ask the tourism bureau about Springfield wine estate, trendy Bon Cap, where they grow organic wines; game viewing at Pat Busch Private Nature Reserve; walks in the Vrolijkheid Nature Reserve; Breede Valley Wines at Branewynsdraai Restaurant where you can buy wines of the region at cellar prices; 4x4 routes; rock climbing at Cogmans Kloof; mountain biking and hiking trails; canoeing and fishing in the Breede River; and fynbos trails in the Dassieshoek Nature Reserve.

Tourism office to De Wetshof – 15min

From the tourism office turn left into Voortrekker Street (the main road out of town). After about 2km, turn right onto the Bonnievale road. You'll pass Springfield (also worth a visit), Viljoensdrift at about 12km, Van Loveren about 2km later, and then turn left into De Wetshof at about 14km.

The Bonnievale road is extraordinarily pretty when the flowers are blooming. A riot of roses gives way to banks of deep red cannas, before an avenue of purple jacarandas leads you up to the De Wetshof tasting room.

If you've explored Cape Town it may look familiar: the tasting room is a replica of the Koopmans de Wet House in Strand Street, the home (now a museum) of the original De Wets who came to South Africa in 1693. Today great-great-great... grandson Danie de Wet makes award-winning chardonnays, along with a wide range of other whites and reds under the De

The hallmark red and white view of Van Loveren

Wetshof, Danie de Wet and Dukesfield labels. Cellar tours by appointment only, phone and book.

Why is Van Loveren especially popular on Saturdays? That's when the wine tasting is accompanied by the legendary Aunty Jean's sweetcorn fritters. Although she is no longer around to make them, her recipe is still followed faithfully to complement the broad range of red and white wines, all well priced for South African budgets.

The tastings are held either in her former home or in her beautiful garden – ask about the delightful stories behind each tree, planted by Aunty Jean to commemorate everything from the end of World War Two, to Mandela's presidency, to family graduations – they read like a potted history of the world! There are no official cellar tours, but you're welcome to stroll through the cellar on your own. And you can bring your own picnic to enjoy in the garden.

During the week you can taste Viljoensdrift wines at the cellar, but even better over weekends is to board *Uncle Ben* and taste everything from chenin blanc, chardonnay and shiraz to merlot and rosé as you chug gently along the Breede River, watching

AUNTIE JEAN'S SWEETCORN FRITTERS

Mix 500g self-raising flour, 2t baking powder, 1t salt, 2 beaten eggs, 2x340g tins of sweetcorn and 3 cups milk together, deep-fry in oil and enjoy!

the birds and soaking up the tranquillity. If you're feeling peckish, the Viljoensdrift team can put together a picnic of pâtés, breads, cheeses, smoked salmon and cold meats to enjoy as you loll on the banks of the river, or to eat on the boat (complete with gingham cloths; book in advance). There are regular riverside concerts on summer Sundays and the odd one in winter where the proceeds go to charity. Groups of 15 or more can hire *Uncle Ben* during the week. But if the water isn't for you, head for the hills and some fine dining at Fraai Uitzicht 1798.

Viljoensdrift to Fraai Uitzicht 1798 – 10min

Turn onto the Bonnievale road towards Robertson, then right to Klaas Voogdsstasie, Ashton, opposite Bon Courage. T-junction right on the Ashton road (R60), then left to Klaas Voogds East (gravel).

You'll feel a happy calm wash over you as you arrive at Fraai Uitzicht 1798, where an abundance of water and brilliantly coloured flowers lead to the restaurant deck, offering stunning views over the whole Robertson valley. Host Axel Spanholtz exudes warm bonhomie, while chef Mario Motti produces the fine food made with herbs and vegetables from the kitchen garden that made the restaurant one of *Wine* Magazine's Top 100 in South Africa.

Take a walk through the vineyards and fruit orchards, or (if they're not too busy) tour the oldest wine cellar in the valley. And if it's just too beautiful to leave, you can spend the night in one of several luxury chalets in the garden. There are concerts every second Wednesday evening.

Fraai Uitzicht 1798 to Soekershof – 7min

Head back down to the R60 and turn right towards Robertson. Turn right to Klaas Voogds West (gravel).

You're cheerfully invited to get lost the moment you arrive at the Soekershof ('Seeker's Court') Walkabout. And that you will, lost both in the various mazes that sprawl over the property, and in the imaginations of the owners, Herman van Bon and Yvonne de Wit, who've created a vast, whimsical garden where it's difficult to tell truth from fantasy. The Dutch pair fell in love with the area while on holiday, and within months had immigrated and bought

FOR THE BIRDS

Take the kids to Birds of Paradise in Robertson, a feathered rainbow of exotic colour, with monkeys, llamas and crocodiles. There's also a Fairy Garden, pony rides and a restaurant.

this sadly neglected property. As they cleared the weeds a fabulously diverse cactus garden began to appear (planted by Maarten Malherbe, a pioneer of the cactus trade in South Africa). From there, as Herman says, 'the project went hopelessly out of control'. They've restored the garden, which now has up to 4 000 different plants, including 1 800 cacti and succulents, and planted a 13 870 square metre hedge maze, the largest in the world. That led to the making of even more mazes, including an ancient Cretan labyrinth of cacti, and an inspiring Philosophers' Garden. Look out for a huge cactus that might be the first ever planted in South Africa. Herman is a master storyteller, who can even work James Bond into the story of Klaas Voogds, the legendary adventurer after whom the area is named, who was finally trampled by an elephant. Be sure to ask what happened to the elephant – but be prepared to suspend belief...

Soekershof to Kolgans – 30 min

Turn right onto the R60 and drive back through Robertson. At about 14.8km,

turn left to Goree. The road becomes gravel at about 19km.
Keep going and turn left to Kolgans at about 24km.

As the sun begins to paint the vineyards orange and the towering mountains purple, follow the narrow track that weaves down to the river on the farm Nerina. At the end is a peaceful inlet, where you board the Kolgans riverboat for a two-hour cruise, gliding quietly among the birds as you enjoy real country food – 'We cook in Afrikaans,' says Amanda Conradie, who runs Kolgans with her husband Frans and family. 'We're not rich or sophisticated, we just love our farm, and we'd like to share it with you.' Bread is baked in jam tins every day, the food is simple and wholesome, and your hosts begin to feel like old friends. And here's a guarantee: as the river unfolds like a ribbon and the silence settles over the valley, you'll find yourself revisiting those fantasies of selling up and moving to the country.

The riverboat offers brunch, lunch, sundowners and dinner, and they'll tailor the trip to suit your timing. Booking essential.

Kolgans to Cape Town – 1hr 35min

Turn right out of Kolgans. At 5km, turn left to Worcester. T-junction left onto tar, R60 Worcester. Retrace your morning route back to Cape Town and the Waterfront.

Mid-summer landscape after the harvest

VITAL INFO

BIRDS OF PARADISE 023 626 3926, daily 9:00–17:00, see www.route62.co.za under attractions

BON CAP ORGANIC WINE 023 626 1628, daily 8:00–17:00, www.boncaporganic.co.za

BREEDE RIVER WINELANDS TOURISM Ashton 023 615 1100

DE WETSHOF ESTATE 023 615 1853, Mon–Fri 8:30–16:30, Sat 9:30–12:30, www.dewetshof.com

FRAAI UITZICHT 1798 023 626 6156, Wed–Sun breakfast, lunch and dinner, www.fraaiuitzicht.com

GRAHAM BECK WINES 023 626 1214, Mon–Fri 9:00–17:00, Sat 10:00–15:00, www.grahambeckwines.co.za

KOLGANS RIVER RESTAURANT 023 626 2012, 082 823 4231, daily brunch, lunch and dinner – they'll change times to accommodate bookings

ROBERTSON TOURISM BUREAU 023 626 4437, www.robertson.org.za

ROBERTSON WINE VALLEY 023 626 3167, www.robertsonwinevalley.co.za

SOEKERSHOF MAZE AND BOTANICAL GARDEN 023 626 4134, Wed–Sun 8:00–16:00, Mon & Tues by appointment, http://soekershof.com

VAN LOVEREN 023 615 1505, Mon–Fri 8:30–17:00, Sat 9:30–13:00, www.vanloveren.co.za

VILJOENSDRIFT WINES 023 615 1901, Mon–Fri 9:00–16:00, Sat 10:00–14:00, cruises around 11:00 or 12:00, with more in afternoon if bookings, www.viljoensdrift.co.za

ANTIQ

Church Street Antiques Market

THE ROUTE:
Search for hidden delights on the dusty shelves of fabulous shops along Church and Long streets in town, then the harbour-side treasure trove of Kalk Bay.

see MAPS B & C
contact details on pp 96 & 97

TIME: One day

DISTANCE: About 45km to Kalk Bay. Add another 10km if you're continuing on to Simon's Town.

BEST TIME TO GO: Rainy days rule out the open air markets, otherwise anytime. Bear in mind early closing time for the city shops over weekends, so Saturday mornings and weekdays are great, with the bonus of the Groot Constantia antiques market on a Sunday.

antiques

INTRODUCTION

Anyone who loves digging and delving in dusty corners, from the ardent antique dealer to the cheerful junk collector, will find something worthy of a little light shopping along this route. It starts in town and heads to the southern suburbs, with built-in diversions if you're burdened with passengers who don't share your passion for antiquities. Between Groot Constantia and Kalk Bay it follows the Constantia Wine Route and passes Steenberg Golf Estate – perfect places to dump your companions so you can indulge your curiosity at leisure.

READING LIST

✓ Look out for the *Antiques, Collectables and Africana Map* in tourism bureaus and antique stores. Updated every year, it lists good antique shops around Cape Town (and Gauteng), all of which are members of the SA Antique Dealer's Association (SAADA).

✓ A really good reference book is the *Antiques Price Guide 2003* by Judith Miller (Dorling Kindersley), which lists over 8 500 antiques, each with a colour photograph, description and, most temptingly, a ballpark figure (in sterling) of what you might pay for a similar item. Have a look – that dusty dish you bought for a song might be worth a fortune.

antiques

Clarke's Bookshop

Groot Constantia Manor House

THE ROUTE

- Explore the Church Street antique market and Long Street shops in the city centre
- Brunch or lunch at Groot Constantia and visit the Sundays-only antiques and collectables market
- Meander along Kalk Bay Main Road to all the antique shops
- If there's still time, head on to Simon's Town for afternoon tea, a browse and a boat trip

 BEFORE YOU GO

- ✓ Church and Long Street shops and markets are closed on Saturday afternoons and Sundays.
- ✓ The Sundays-only market at Groot Constantia more than makes up for that.
- ✓ Buy yourself a cash card to feed the parking meters in Long Street, or negotiate with one of the parking attendants, who'll make sure you don't run out of time. Costs range from about R2 an hour.

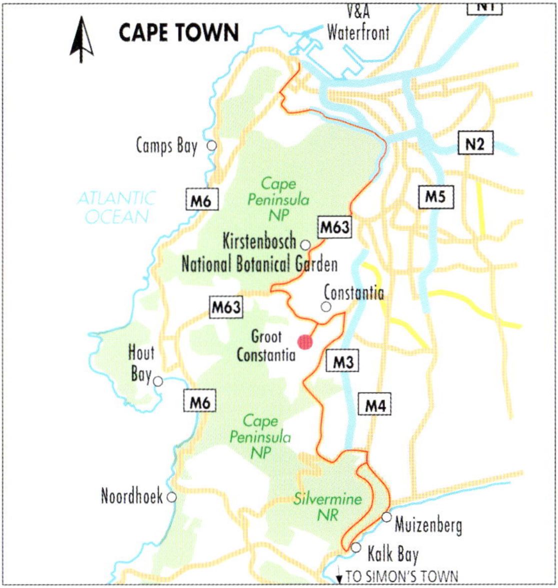

CAPE TOWN

N1

V&A Waterfront

Camps Bay

Cape Peninsula NP

N2

ATLANTIC OCEAN

M6

M5

M63

Kirstenbosch National Botanical Garden

M63

Constantia

Hout Bay

Groot Constantia

M3

M6

M4

Cape Peninsula NP

Noordhoek

Silvermine NR

Muizenberg

Kalk Bay

↓ TO SIMON'S TOWN

V&A WATERFRONT

Wessels

Dock

Duncan

Dock

Somerset

Chiappini

Dixon

Cape Town International Convention Centre

Coen Steytler

Hans Strijdom

Bree

Heerengracht

Shortmarket

Roge

Castle

Waterkant

Church

Loop

Strand

Bo-Kaap

Dorp

Bree

Adderley

Cape Town Station

Civic Centre

Oswald Pirow

N1

Buitengracht

Long

Burg

Greenmarket

Wale

Parliament

Grand Parade

Foreshore

Queen Victoria

Plein

Darling

Castle of Good Hope

Government Ave

Parade

New Market R102

Dormehl

Sir Lowry

District Six Museum

Canterbury

Caledon

Kloof St

Orange

Buitenkant

Roeland

Cape Technikon

Mill

Jutland

De Waal

TO GROOT CONSTANTIA

Bruce Tait Kitsch and Collectables

Waterfront to Church and Long streets – 5min

From the Waterfront turn right into Buitengracht Street (M62 Camps Bay). After 1km turn left into Wale Street, then third right into Long Street and park. Head back down Long Street on foot (against the flow of the one-way traffic), cross Wale Street, Church Street is next. The Church Street Antiques Market, billed as Cape Town's original market, is in the pedestrians-only area to your right. Non-shoppers can enjoy breakfast at one of the pavement tables at Café Mozart, while you wander from stall to stall, each brimming with old china, brilliant brassware, ancient coins, velvet gloves and old jewellery (including rare, and large, Zulu earrings that are inserted into the lobes), bric-a-brac and interesting junk. The market complements some more highbrow antique shops and galleries that are worth visiting in the same street. Keep going to Burr & Muir, an emporium of art nouveau and art deco. Also pop into African Image, on the corner of Church and Burg streets, for beautiful (and some fun) African artefacts, old and new.

Once you've exhausted Church Street, head back up Long Street towards the mountain and look out for the entrance to the Long Street Antique Arcade on your left. (If you hit Wale Street you've gone too far.)

This is a rabbit warren of more than a dozen tiny shops, each well worth a dig. You'll find beautiful old maps and prints dating back to the 1800s, militaria and medals, scientific and medical curiosities straight from the lab, dusty cameras, clocks, ethnic art and silverware, as well as the more predictable jewellery, china, paintings and porcelain.

The arcade cuts the corner of the city block, so you'll pop out onto the pavement in Wale Street. Turn right then left into Long Street, for a meander up one of the most lively and diverse streets in Cape Town.

Here antique and book shops sit sombrely next to backpacker lodges, student pubs, über-trendy fashion boutiques, clubs, pavement restaurants and seriously good cafés. The street is peopled with a lively babble of tourists, grungy students, Rastas, artists and inevitable bergies, and you'll almost certainly trip over a film crew using Long Street as a historical/trendy/inner city backdrop for a shoot.

On your wander up Long Street, look out for Clarke's Bookshop, possibly Cape Town's most important purveyor of rare and out-of-print books on southern Africa (as well as new ones) that tower to the ceiling.

Bristol Antiques is also on this street and a little further on you'll find Atkinson's Antiques for fine jewellery, silverware, watches and objets d'art, as well as Second Time Around, for sequinned vintage and contemporary clothing and costume jewellery you can pick up for a (comparative!) song.

If all the antique dust is getting to you, there's also a factory shop full of outdoor gear for hikers, a couple of trendy fashion stores and one or two beautiful gifty/décor shops. Or settle down with a beer at one of the several pubs and pavement cafés that line Long Street.

Right at the top of Long Street, past the Long Street Baths and across Buitensingel Road, you'll find another retro haven that's a winner with film crews looking for relics of the 50s and 60s. Bruce Tait Kitsch and Collectables, with arguably the most pierced man in Cape Town behind the till, bulges with feather boas, plastic fruit lights and all manner of glorious kitsch and collectables. You'll battle to leave without buying something and if you've always wanted a nodding dog for your rear windscreen, here's the store for you.

Modern kitsch in Kloof Street

Long Street to Groot Constantia – 25min

From the traffic lights at the top of Long Street, turn left into Orange Street and follow signs for N2 Somerset West and M3 Muizenberg to join highway. At Hospital Bend stay right, following signs for M3 Muizenberg and brown signs for Kirstenbosch. At about 10km, turn right into Rhodes Avenue, M63 Hout Bay, passing Kirstenbosch Botanical Gardens after 2km. T-junction right to Hout Bay and Constantia Nek. At 17km on Constantia Nek circle, turn sharp left to Constantia Main Road, M41 Wynberg. Turn right after brown Groot Constantia sign – the entrance to the wine estate is about 500m further.

A sense of history, distant views over False Bay and an antiques market every Sunday make Groot Constantia a good stop for lunch or brunch. The wine estate dates to 1685, when the land was granted to Simon van der Stel, a governor of the Cape. He planted fruit trees, oaks and vines, and about 40 of his vines still thrive here today.

The manor house, built in 1692 at the end of an avenue of stately oaks, is one of the best-preserved examples of Cape Dutch architecture, and it houses a priceless collection of Cape furniture and porcelain.

The original wine cellar, dated 1791, is now a wine museum of drinking utensils and artefacts, including ancient amphoras, delicate glassware and an impressive set of imperial measures from gallon and quart to pint and a half-gill. Their assize stamp is 1569, and they were used at the Cape back in 1875. The

GROOT CONSTANTIA

Groot Constantia is South Africa's oldest wine estate, and its wines have been famous around the world for centuries. They were coveted by the British Royal House, King Louis Philippe of France, Frederick (the Great) of Prussia and others of Europe's eighteenth century aristocracy, and they're even mentioned by Jane Austen in *Sense and Sensibility*. Napoleon Bonaparte, while in exile on St Helena, would drink nothing else.

swimming bath, from around 1795, is a pleasant stroll away from the main buildings. The Sundays-only antiques and collectables market is in a shaded courtyard that used to be part of the estate's old slave quarters. Browse through old china, books, antique and costume jewellery and plenty of shining cutlery and delicate silverware.

Have a meal at one of the two fully licensed restaurants – a general menu and traditional Cape fare at the Jonkershuis (they offer a sampler dish where you can taste a little of everything) or dine on some fine international cuisine, from burgers to venison, at Simon's.

Afterwards, tour the cellar and do a tasting of Groot Constantia's large range of wines – the shop and tasting cellar

is on the left just before you drive out of the estate's main gate. Cellar tours every hour in summer, three per day in winter time.

Groot Constantia to Kalk Bay – 25min

From Groot Constantia turn right onto Constantia Main Road, M41 Wynberg. At 1.5km turn right at traffic lights into Ladies Mile Road, M39 Bergvliet. At next lights turn right onto M42 Tokai. Follow the Constantia Wine Route past Buitenverwachting, Klein Constantia and Steenberg Wine and Golf Estate. Go straight through two traffic lights as the road curves along the foot of the mountain. (At around 11km you'll pass the end of the M3 highway, which will later be your direct route back to the city.) At 11.8km, T-junction right into Main Road, M4 Muizenberg. Follow the railway line through Muizenberg and St James to Kalk Bay.

As you turn onto the Main Road, which was the old wagon road between the Castle in Cape Town and Muizenberg, you'll see one of the original carved milestones on your right, showing it's 13 miles to the Town Hall. Ancient Days Antiques, on the left shortly after you join the Main Road, is also worth a stop for interesting furniture, especially yellowwood farm pieces. If you were able to resist the temptation to stop at the various estates along the Constantia Wine Route, Kalk Bay delivers a main street full of quirky shops and eateries, all filled with the sound of screeching seagulls and breaking waves.

A lingering exploration of all of them is highly recommended, with a break for tea in the middle if your credit card is smoking. (But if you've seen enough antiques to last a lifetime, browse the various art galleries or watch the waves over a glass of wine at the Brass Bell restaurant on Kalk Bay station.)

Better still, have a meal at Cape to Cuba above Kalk Bay Harbour and shop from your table. Meet Cape Town's very own Che Guevara reincarnated as an antique shop owner in a restaurant packed with Madonna statues, astonishingly lavish chandeliers and ornate metal furniture, all with a price tag attached so you can add what you like to your bill.

A magpie meander turned up these temptations in Kalk Bay:
- Spices in brown bags for sale amid the collectables in Shor Bazaar, named after the 'thieves market' in Bombay
- A set of Thomas Baines prints at Graciously Ancient
- A weird mix of antique furniture, peppered with African artefacts, at two shops in one building – Belle Ombre Antiques and African Art
- Ballot papers from South Africa's first democratic election in 1994, juke boxes and old Cape furniture at The Railway House
- A very bad place for bulls, amid thousands of plates and more at The What Not and China Town
- Tram benches, a brass ship's foghorn, old toys and official red post boxes in the Kalk Bay Trading Post at the old post office
- Vintage wine and jewellery at the Kalk Bay Antiques Centre
- Magnificent clocks and fancy leather top hat boxes at Tim Curtis Antiques
- Cries of London prints on the wall at Cries of London
- Art, books, Africana and very old bones at Quagga Trading
- Africana, a beautiful roll-top desk and suitably ancient African masks in the dim interior of the Treasure Trove
  If time permits, head for historic Simon's Town for some

maritime memorabilia or even a boat trip – simply remain on the Main Road for another nine kilometres, keeping the sea to your left all the way.

Kalk Bay to Waterfront – 40min

Turn into Boyes Drive, M75 Clairvaux Road at the traffic lights near the entrance to the harbour. This scenic 7km route takes you back to the Main Road opposite the Westlake Wetlands. At the T-junction turn left onto Main Road, M4 Retreat, then left into Steenberg Road, M42 Westlake, M3 Cape Town. Turn onto highway at the first lights and follow M3 Cape Town signs to the Waterfront.

ANTIQUES ON OTHER ROUTES

- ✓ Stanford on the Whale Route, see pp 186–187
- ✓ Franschhoek on the Wine Route, see p 47
- ✓ Simon's Town as well as Hout Bay on the Big Hits Route, see pp 25 & 29
- ✓ Claremont, Kloof Street and De Waterkant on the Art & Desirables Route, see pp 98–111

Kalk Bay meander

VITAL INFO

CHURCH STREET

AFRICAN IMAGE cnr Church & Burg streets, 021 423 8385

CHURCH STREET ANTIQUES MARKET 021 438 8566, Mon–Sat 8:30–14:00 (but they pack up earlier on Saturdays)

LONG STREET ANTIQUE ARCADE 021 423 3585, Mon–Fri 9:00–17:00, Sat 9:00–14:00

LONG STREET

These shops generally follow business hours of 9:00–17:00 weekdays, closing at lunch time on Saturdays, while the restaurants and clubs go on way into the night.

ATKINSON'S ANTIQUES 021 424 3726

BRISTOL ANTIQUES 021 424 2647

BRUCE TAIT KITSCH AND COLLECTABLES Kloof Street, 021 422 1567

CLARKE'S BOOKSHOP 021 423 5739

SECOND TIME AROUND 021 423 1674

KALK BAY MAIN ROAD

These shops are generally open daily 9:00–17:00.

Some open at 10:00 on Sundays.

BELLE OMBRE ANTIQUES & AFRICAN ART 021 788 9802

CAPE TO CUBA 021 788 1566, daily 11:30–16:00, 18:00–approx 23:00

CRIES OF LONDON 021 788 3256

GRACIOUSLY ANCIENT 021 788 5577

Classy collectables at Pieter Visser

VITAL INFO

KALK BAY ANTIQUES CENTRE 021 788 8882
KALK BAY TRADING POST 021 788 9571
QUAGGA TRADING 021 788 2752
SHOR BAZAAR 021 788 7113
THE RAILWAY HOUSE 021 788 4761
THE WHAT NOT AND CHINA TOWN 021 788 1823
TIM CURTIS ANTIQUES 021 788 8701
TREASURE TROVE 021 788 4802

GROOT CONSTANTIA
CELLAR TOURS hourly from 10:00–16:00 (in winter at 10, 11 and 15:00),
Tasting and sales daily 9:00–17:00
GROOT CONSTANTIA ANTIQUE AND COLLECTABLES MARKET 021 689 3908,
083 324 9264, Sun 10:00–16:30
GROOT CONSTANTIA ESTATE 021 794 5128 or 794 5067
JONKERSHUIS RESTAURANT Groot Constantia, 021 794 6255,
Tues–Sat 9:00–22:30, Sun–Mon 9:00–16:30
MANOR HOUSE AND MUSEUM daily 10:00–17:00
SIMON'S Groot Constantia, 021 794 1143, daily 11:00–22:30

ALL THE REST
ANCIENT DAYS ANTIQUES Main Road, Retreat, 021 788 6450, closed Sat
CAFÉ MOZART Church Street, 021 424 3774, Mon–Fri 7:00–3:15,
Sat 8:00–13:00

Ethnic beaded jewellry

THE ROUTE:
Shop – yes, till you drop – for beautiful things in galleries and other emporiums of the deeply desirable, in De Waterkant, Long Street, Kloof Street, Newlands and Claremont.
see MAPS B & C
contact details on p 110

TIME: One day

DISTANCE: 25km, round trip

BEST TIME TO GO: Whenever you've got money in your pocket (and especially when you haven't) – nothing like a little light shopping to perk you up.

art & desirables

INTRODUCTION

This is a route of beautiful things – be it oil on a canvas, a swirl of beads on a designer dress, or the sparkle on handcrafted silverware.

With the emphasis on local is lekker, we rounded up the fearlessly fashion conscious and the doyennes of the deeply desirable, to help find the most satisfying emporiums of covetable goodies, from art galleries to gift shops, from fashion designers to master crafters. Call it retail therapy, call it the pursuit of beauty – whatever it is, it's not for sissies. We're packing in a lot here: be warned that this route is aimed at committed shoppers ready to go the distance. So slip into your most comfy pair of shoes, and keep up!

 READING LIST

✓ Get hold of the *House & Leisure Arts & Crafts* Cape Town map, with maps and listings of galleries and shops in the city centre and the Cape.

✓ For absolutely every outlet offering a discount, consult *Pam Black's A–Z of Factory Shops in the Western Cape* (Pam Black Publications).

art & Desirables

Traditional Garment

Green Point flea market

THE ROUTE

- Breakfast and browsing around the Cape Quarter and De Waterkant

- A quick zip into the city centre, Shortmarket, Church, Long and Kloof streets

- Lunch at Montebello Craft and Design Centre, Newlands

- The afternoon at Cavendish Square, Claremont

DON'T MISS THE MARKETS

- ✓ Pan African Market – go from Cape to Cairo in one building (76 Long St)

- ✓ Greenmarket Square – for clothing and curios (Burg St)

- ✓ Church St Antiques Market – clothes, crockery, coins and more (Church St)

- ✓ Green Point Flea Market on Sundays – a car-boot sale on a massive scale

- ✓ Blue and Red Sheds at the Waterfront – for everything under the sun

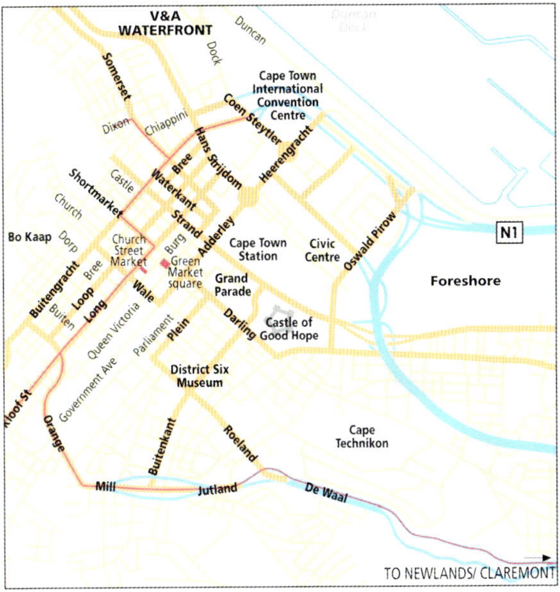

Map 1 (Cape Town City Centre)

V&A WATERFRONT

Duncan Dock

Somerset
Dixon
Chiappini
Castle
Shortmarket
Church
Bo Kaap
Dorp
Church Street Market
Buitengracht
Bree
Buiten
Long
Loop
Queen Victoria
Kloof St
Orange
Government Ave
Mill
Buitenkant
Jutland

Coen Steytler
Cape Town International Convention Centre
Hans Strijdom
Bree
Waterkant
Strand
Burg
Adderley
Green Market square
Wale
Parliament
Plein
District Six Museum
Roeland
De Waal

Heerengracht
Cape Town Station
Grand Parade
Darling
Castle of Good Hope

Civic Centre
Oswald Pirow
Foreshore
N1

Cape Technikon

TO NEWLANDS/ CLAREMONT

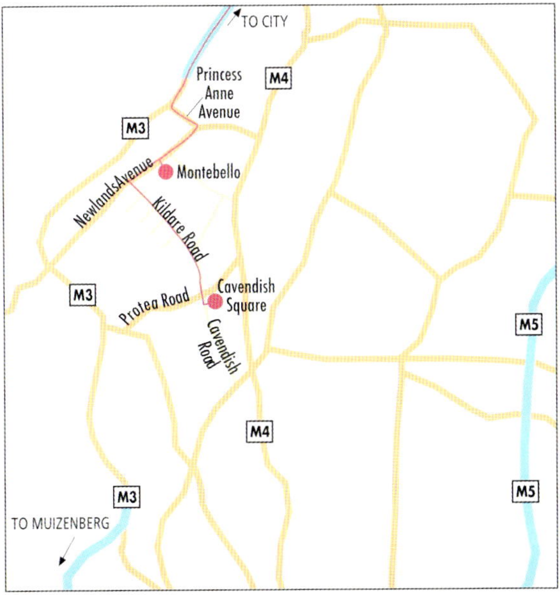

Map 2

TO CITY
M4
Princess Anne Avenue
M3
Newlands Avenue
Montebello
Kildare Road
M3
Protea Road
Cavendish Square
Cavendish Road
M4
M3
M5
M5
TO MUIZENBERG

Greenmarket Square

Waterfront to De Waterkant – 4min

From the Waterfront turn right into Buitengracht. At the second lights turn right into Somerset Road. At about 500m, turn left into Dixon Road and left into the Cape Quarter.

The lift from the underground parking delivers you into a delightfully different world – at the heart of the Cape Quarter is a piazza, complete with sparkling fountain and café tables, ringed with an enchanting variety of shops. Fortify yourself with a good breakfast on the square (or there's the fabulously French La Petite Tarte, with hibiscus and mallow teas, facing the street) before the shopping spree.

Make a point of popping into Africa Nova – all original African contemporary handmade art, including beautiful beads, fabrics, paper, jewellery and ceramics, and not a curio in sight. East of Eden is an eclectic mix of Asian kitsch and cool, with funky Icuba clothing as well. For the sheer majesty and scale of

INSIDER TRADING

Traditional home of the rag trade, Cape Town has factory shops for several desirable famous brands:

- ✓ Zoom shoes, 18 Auckland Street, Paarden Eiland
- ✓ Hip Hop, 39 Roeland Street, Cape Town
- ✓ Green Cross, 26 Benbow Avenue, Epping Industria
- ✓ Polo, Shop A6, Access Park, Kenilworth
- ✓ Speedo, Bofors Circle, Epping Industria

the pieces, have a look at Private Collections (part of Old Colonial). It's a huge shop of mainly Indian antiques and 'architectural pieces', like entire doorways, which must have come from maharajahs' palaces.

Walk out at Vos Lane and cross the road to India Jane, for spangled fashion from various designers (all beautifully grouped by colour), gorgeous shoes and some lifestyle gear, with A Suitable Boy above it – more of the same but for the boys.

Keep going down Waterkant Street (towards the city) for about two blocks (it may well look as if you're heading into car mechanic land, but keep going!) to the 3rd i Gallery of modern contemporary art – 'it's what people are creating now', say owners Sharon Peers (photographer) and Chantal Coetzee (artist), who exhibit their own and other artists' work. Head back to the Cape Quarter, cross through it (or pick up your car) and go along Jarvis Street to De Smidt Street. Inside Hill House is the Michael Stevenson Contemporary Gallery, one of the must-sees on the Cape Town art route, which hosts changing exhibitions from award-winning artists.

Turn right into Somerset Street to get to the city centre, but be sure to stop at Plush Bazaar on the right – a splendidly whimsical place of antique glasses, mirrors, chandeliers and lovely Victorian garden things.

Somerset Street to Riebeeck Square – 4min

Turn right back into Buitengracht. Turn left into Kortmark (Shortmarket Street) and park on Riebeeck Square.

Parking in town can be tricky, so abandon the car and walk. Cross Buitengracht and head (again among vehicle workshops) up Shortmarket to Streetwires, full of wizards who can make whatever you fancy out of wire. They're equally unfazed by orders for beaded chameleons or 2.5 metre high baobabs (destined for Kirstenbosch Botanical Garden). Walk back across Riebeeck Square down to Long Street, then head

Canvasses and art supplies

right for two blocks (past the 30 stalls in one building of the Pan African Craft Market) to Church Street, another delicious mecca for lovers of beautiful things.

Look around AVA (Association for Visual Arts), a non-profit dynamic gallery that showcases local contemporary work and has a shop selling pieces from recent exhibitions, and the Peanut Gallery across the road and upstairs, for more 'affordable art'. The Peter Visser Gallery – ceramics in the basement, antiques on the ground floor and framed art up a tiny spiral staircase – faces Peter Visser Gifts, where among other covetable goodies you'll find a huge selection of Carrol Boyes pewter cutlery and gifts. African Image has an eclectic and cheerful mix of African artefacts and local fun stuff too.

You may want to get your car now for a slow trawl up Long Street – peep into Bohemian Lifestyle for voluptuously pretty textiles and fantastic fairy lights, Still Life, an emporium of furniture and décor, and Mememe for an edgy mix of fashion and art. Opposite Long Street Café, turn right up Buiten Street to the Bell-Roberts Art Gallery (on the corner of Loop Street) for über cool graphic art, a coffee shop and art bookstore (the business card folds up into a little box – how's that for graphic?).

Cross Buitensingel and keep going up Kloof Street – if your credit card isn't smoking by now, it soon will be.

Check out Bruce Tait Kitsch and Collectables, and So Now? which mixes fashion and art. There's also the Photographers Gallery, with the Lim (Less Is More) and Klooftique furniture and

textile showrooms underneath, then Lim (the gift shop). Look out for Ottigers near Melissa's (an excellent spot for coffee and a bite to eat), and Hotchi-Witchi for all things old and collectable, from kitchenware to cameras.

You must stop at Heartworks, set slightly back on the corner of De Lorentz Street. It's a rainbow of quirky African arts and crafts, from bright beads and bags to delicate poppy and petunia-shaped cups and saucers from Kate Carlyle's Mustardseed and Moonshine range. Everything is sourced 'south of the Zambezi and nothing over wavy water', says owner Margaret Woermann. Marx & Harris is just a few shops further up – lovely décor and handmade, handwrapped soaps. Right near the top of Kloof is Loft Living, the last word in décor.

Kloof Street to Montebello – 15min

Turn back down Kloof Street and into Rheede Street, opposite Vida e Caffè – the best muffins in town! Turn right at traffic lights into Orange Street; keep following M3 Muizenberg till you join the highway. At 8km take Exit 8, M146 Princess Anne Avenue and turn left to Newlands. Get into right lane immediately, and turn right into Newlands Avenue. Turn left into Montebello at 9km.

The beautiful cast-iron filigreed fence around Montebello hides a cool and quiet oasis of artists' studios, jewellers, mosaic makers, ceramicists and a Bushman craft shop, housed in elegant old buildings that were once stables and a cowshed for the nearby homestead.

There's also an old-fashioned glass greenhouse attached to a nursery, with a blacksmith's forge at the back. Have lunch under the shady trees at the Gardener's Cottage, then wander around the studios to watch buyable art in the making – look out for fine artists and printmakers Alma Ita Vorster and Judy Woodbourne who are based here.

Montebello to Cavendish Square – 5min

From Montebello turn left into Newlands Avenue. At 400m turn left into Kildare Road. Pass Melissa's deli, Elzbieta Rosenwerth (fashion) and L'Orangerie (décor). Cross Protea Road at 1.4km and turn left into Cavendish Square parking at 1.6km.

108

And this is where we'll leave you, confident that there's something at Cavendish to delight even the most footsore shopper or discerning art lover. Make a point though of looking in at the Young Designers Emporium, an innovative concept store created by entrepreneur Paul Simon, who realised young local designers needed a showcase for their fashion. So you'll find loads and loads of on-the-edge labels from fashion gurus in the making (but please know that they cater for skinny people only).

Paul Simon then took it further with Bread and Butter around the corner. He and art curator Kim Stern have created an art-gift store where they sell delightful off-the-wall graphic goodies made by local artists – the 'bread-and-butter' work that finances their more serious art. It's whacky stuff – you too can have the best-dressed ironing board on the planet.

End the day with dinner or a movie, or just keep shopping – stores stay open till 18:00 during the week, 21:00 on Fridays and Saturdays, but close at 16:00 on Sundays.

Cavendish Square to Waterfront – 15min

Take the Vineyard Road parking exit and turn left. Turn right into Cavendish Street, then left into Protea. Turn right at the circle. At the traffic lights turn right into Edinburgh Drive, following M3 Cape Town. At Hospital Bend veer right, and follow the signs back to the Waterfront.

beads

3RD i GALLERY 95 Waterkant Street, 021 425 2266

CAPE QUARTER cnr Dixon & Waterkant streets, Green Point, 021 421 0737

INDIA JANE (also in Kalk Bay and Claremont), 021 421 3517/8

MICHAEL STEVENSON CONTEMPORARY GALLERY Hill House, De Smidt Street, 021 421 2575

PAN AFRICAN MARKET 76 Long Street, 021 426 4478

PLUSH BAZAAR 30 Somerset Road, 021 419 8328

STREETWIRES 77/79 Shortmarket Street, 021 426 2475

AROUND CHURCH STREET

AFRICAN IMAGE 021 423 8385

ASSOCIATION FOR VISUAL ARTS 021 424 7436

PEANUT GALLERY 021 426 5404

PETER VISSER GALLERY 021 423 7870

PETER VISSER GIFTS 021 422 2660

KLOOF STREET

BRUCE TAIT KITSCH & COLLECTABLES 021 422 4567

HEARTWORKS (also Gardens Centre), 021 424 8419

HOTCHI-WITCHI 021 422 3811

KLOOFTIQUE 021 424 9458

LIM 021 423 1200

LOFT LIVING 021 423 1465

MARX & HARRIS 021 422 3980

OTTIGER'S 021 422 5528

PHOTOGRAPHERS GALLERY 021 422 2762

SO NOW? 021 422 5085

LONG STREET

BOHEMIAN LIFESTYLE 021 422 4462

MEMEME 021 424 0001

STILL LIFE 021 426 0143

CLAREMONT/NEWLANDS

MONTEBELLO CRAFT & DESIGN CENTRE 31 Newlands Avenue, 021 685 6445

CAVENDISH SQUARE SHOPPING CENTRE Claremont, 021 674 3050

One of the few ornate entrances in Cape Town.

Outdoor amusement at Spier

THE ROUTE:

Indoor fun for rainy days, with ideas around the Peninsula and Somerset West for when the sun comes out.

see MAPS B & C

contact details on pp 124 & 125

TIME: One day

DISTANCE: About 45km

BEST TIME TO GO:
Any time, but busier during local school holidays in December, January, June and July.

kids

INTRODUCTION

There's no shortage of things to occupy the kids when the sun's shining, but what about when the weather won't play along? Before everyone starts climbing the walls, head under cover for some adrenalin-charged action-climbing and ice-skating, with some educational bits in between.

In case you're travelling in other directions, we have included more options along the N1, around the Cape Peninsula and along the N2 in Somerset West, plus some outdoor stuff for when the weather's being more obliging.

All these venues are guaranteed to banish adult boredom as well. So go on, release your inner child...

BEFORE YOU GO

✓ This route is geared for children aged five years and older, with no upper age limit.

✓ City Rock is closed in the mornings (although this may change, so phone to check).

✓ No kids under five at City Rock, for safety reasons.

✓ GrandWest's ice-rink has morning and afternoon sessions, but is closed daily 12:00–14:00 for resurfacing and private training.

✓ The Magic Castle is normally closed Mon–Thurs, but opens during school holidays.

The Cobra at Ratanga Junction

Static electricity
at the MTN ScienCentre

THE ROUTE

- Ice-skating (or whatever!) at GrandWest Casino and Entertainment World
- Mind-boggling stuff at the MTN ScienCentre in Canal Walk, Century City
- Indoor climbing at City Rock, Observatory
- If your kids are too young to climb, head back to the Waterfront for fun at the Two Oceans Aquarium, Scratch Patch, Telkom Exploratorium, Cyberworld or Imax.

WHERE ELSE CAN YOU TAKE THE KIDS?

✓ For a great day trip that'll keep you and the kids happy, try Spier wine estate near Stellenbosch. You enjoy the fine wine and excellent food in gorgeous surroundings (see Wine Route, pp 43–44), while the kids get up close and personal with several beautiful cheetahs. Alongside is Eagle Encounters, a raptor rehab centre, where you can see 'Mum', the spotted eagle owl who's raising generations of orphans, or come face to face with martial eagles, vultures and falcons.

✓ But the real highlight is the Children's Garden at Spier, created to give 'children a real experience of nature, to try and touch their souls,' says project director Avril Thomson. There's a flying fox slide, a treehouse, an arts and crafts area, a rock for climbing and an enchanted garden. In peak season and over weekends you'll find stiltwalkers towering over the kids, and various performances in the amphitheatre. Aimed at toddlers to teens under 14.

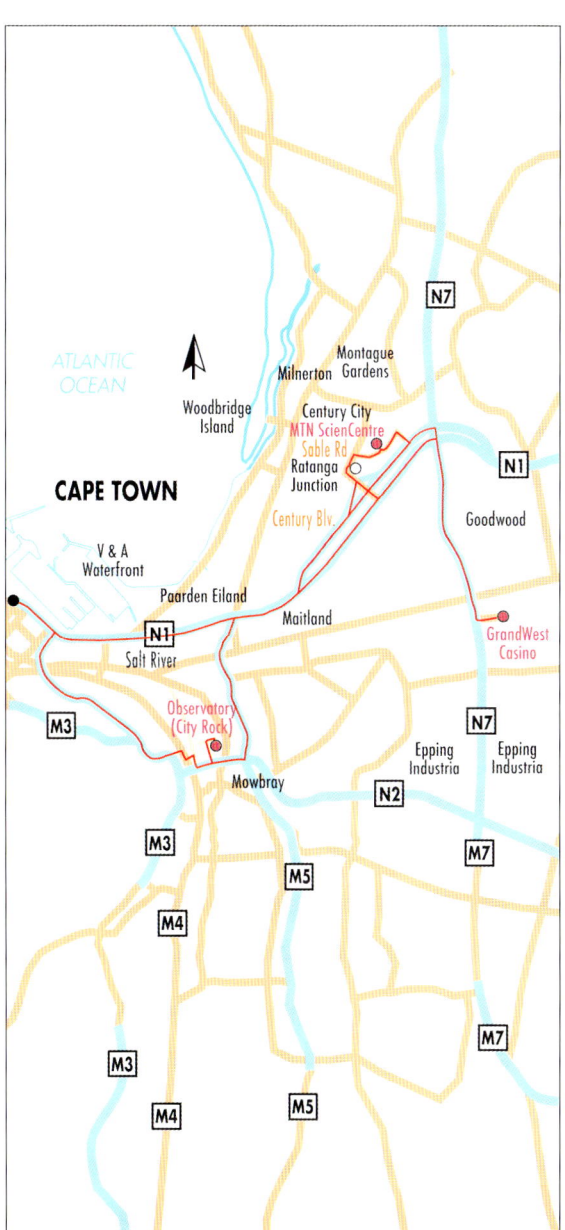

Waterfront to GrandWest Casino & Entertainment World – 20min

From Waterfront turn left, following signs for N1 Paarl. At 7km, take Exit 10 to Sable Road, Century City. Keep straight past Century City, following signs to N7 Goodwood. At 11km, take Exit 13B to Goodwood – the road curves around to join the N7 highway. Go straight through three traffic lights. At 15km take exit to Thornton, Epping, then turn left at the traffic lights into casino.

Mention a magic village of Barbie Doll World, LegoWorld and Lion King World and kids will feel they've hit the jackpot. This is fantasy land for both adults and kids; it's fake but fun.

Best of all is the Olympic-size ice-skating rink, and a separate mini-rink for the very small ones, with tables all round so you can keep an eye on them. Boots for hire start with bob skates (a skate with double blades, strapped to the shoe) at baby size eight and go up to adults' sizes.

A vast games arcade leads you to The Magic Castle, which has mini Putt-Putt and loads of fairground attractions like bumper cars and a carousel, as well as a go-kart track if you're 1.5 metres or taller. (Children under 10 years must be accompanied by an adult.) The Magic Village has themed 'worlds' and a monstrous jungle gym, where kids are supervised and entertained. Note that children are not allowed near the gaming areas, so if you want

WHAT ELSE IS NEARBY?

✓ Ratanga Junction – the largest theme park in Africa. Closed in winter.

✓ Sanccob, the world-famous rescue centre for injured or oil-soaked coastal birds. The penguin feeds at 10:00 and 15:00 are great to watch.

✓ West Coast Ostrich Ranch. Learn about these birds, sit on one, and try standing on one of their huge eggs.

✓ Tygerberg Zoo and endangered wildlife breeding centre – see who's who at the zoo.

some kid-free time while you try your luck on the tables and machines, there is a crèche for children under four years, or supervised care and extra security in the Magic Village, where sensors are clipped to the child's clothing, and the entire area is covered by closed-circuit TV.

GrandWest to MTN ScienCentre, Canal Walk – 25min

Leave GrandWest and turn right under the highway to join it (N7 Malmesbury). At 4km, take Exit 13A, N1 Cape Town. At 6km take Exit 10 Sableweg, turn right at the lights and cross over the highway. Ratanga Junction will be on your right. At 8km, turn right at the traffic lights into Century Boulevard. Aim for Entrance 5 of the Canal Walk shopping centre and park on the roof. The ScienCentre is situated in Shop 407.

If you've ever wondered what you'd weigh on Mars, the answer's at the MTN ScienCentre, an awesome, hands-on playground where you can do some really cool stuff, like experience what it's like to walk (or rather boiing) around on the moon, or play a symphony on a laser harp with no strings. You can land a satellite in the space simulator, watch yourself in a zero-gravity mirror, and find out why wheels don't have to be round. This is fun stuff for all ages and even three-year-olds will enjoy the construction site. The space race spawned a variety of handy gizmos we know today, such as tinfoil, cordless drills for EVA (extravehicular activity) and digital watches. NASA also developed a space pen, so that American astronauts could write upside-down and in zero gravity. The Russians simply used pencils!

MTN ScienCentre to City Rock – 25min

Follow exit signs to N1 Cape Town and retrace your route past Ratanga Junction and onto the highway into the city. At 5km, take Exit 7A, M5 Muizenberg. Keep right as the road splits, following M5 Muizenberg. At about 8km, take Exit 9B N2 Cape Town, curve around and join N2. At 10km, take Exit 8, Liesbeek Parkway. At the traffic light, turn right under the bridge (M57 North). At 11km, after stadium, turn left into Station Road. Cross bridge, turn right into Drake Street and right again into Collingwood Road. City Rock is the last building on the right.

OK, now you're allowed to climb the walls. After squeezing into a harness and clipping onto a safety line, there are 450 square metres of wall (and ceiling), dotted with hand- and footholds, waiting for you at City Rock, South Africa's largest indoor climbing gym. The different routes are graded from easy to (almost) impossible, and there's a dedicated beginners' and kids' wall. Or you can try scrambling up a range of 'boulders', with the comfort of very thick mats at the bottom.

WHILE THE KIDS ARE BUSY...

The MTN ScienCentre is pretty noisy so you might want to leave the kids there while you explore Canal Walk, one of Cape Town's most glamorous and glossy shopping malls. The ScienCentre has facilitators on the floor keeping an eye on things, and security at the exits.

You don't have to be an experienced Spiderman to have fun here. Two-hour beginners' courses are available, or you can hire staff to belay you (keep you secure on the safety rope as you climb), and they'll help you with technique too. This is guaranteed to get the adrenalin pumping, even for kids who feel no fear! And, adults, give it a go – you will definitely love the thrill.

City Rock is owned and run by experienced climbers, and there's a strong emphasis on safety. Hire gear or bring your own. This is also a great place for kids' birthday parties, and there are special programmes during school holidays. The climbs are graded from an eight (which anyone would be able to do) to a white-knuckled 32 – so far only one person has managed to do that climb. Grown-ups, if you feel you now deserve a stiff drink after this kid-friendly day, there are several good restaurants and pubs along Lower Main Road in bohemian Observatory. Otherwise head back to the Waterfront where there's lots more to do for both kids and their parents.

City Rock, Observatory to V&A Waterfront – 7min

City Rock

From City Rock turn left into Drake Street then right into Station Road. At traffic lights, left into Lower Main Road. At around 600m, turn right into Bowden Road and cross Main Road. At 1km, take the left fork onto the bridge, and

turn right at the stop street to City/Stad. Join the highway and follow the signs to the Waterfront.

The great outdoors

When the weather's too good to waste indoors, get out and enjoy the sunshine (but don't forget the sunblock).

Outside action: Head for the hills and enjoy the sunshine on easy walks on the mountain, from Silvermine to Table Mountain.

- Around the Cape Peninsula, try Groot Constantia, where there's plenty of space to roar around while you enjoy lunch (see Antiques Route, pp 91–93), or Kirstenbosch Botanical Garden for picnics, lawns for games, nature walks and ducks on the ponds (see Big Hits Route, pp 21–22).
- But for some real action, get hooked up to a cable for a 900 metre waterski around the lake (or wakeboarding and slalom) at Blue Rock in Somerset West. There's also freshwater scuba-diving, beach volleyball, mini golf, a restaurant and a children's playground.

Beach babies: Pack a picnic, brolly and loads of sunscreen and head for the beach. Boulders, past Simon's Town, offers safe, calm bathing amid huge boulders, with penguins to keep

kids

Two Oceans Aquarium

you entertained. (Entrance fee charged.) More safe seas at Fish Hoek, with rock pools to explore off Jager Walk and jungle gym near the restaurant (have a meal while the kids let off steam). Surfer's Corner at Muizenberg attracts board riders of all ages, with miles of beach and safe swimming. Don't forget the tidal pools at St James, Kommetjie and Dalebrook. Closer to town there are several places to access the beach along the Sea Point beach front, although the shoreline's a bit rocky.

Furry and feathered friends: If you're travelling out towards Stellenbosch and Paarl, look out for a variety of wild beasties, all fairly close to the N1 highway, at the Drakenstein Lion Park, Butterfly World, Le Bonheur Croc Park, Animal Zone and Tygerberg Zoo. (See the Cheese Route on p 66 for details.)

- Ride a camel at Imhoff's Country Craft Farm in Kommetjie, or head to Hout Bay's World of Birds, where you can see over 3 000 birds in natural surroundings. And on a slightly larger scale, have a look at South Africa's biggest bird at the Cape Point Ostrich Farm.
- Up the N2 to Somerset West, stop at Monkey Town, a primate rehabilitation centre, to come face to face with our closest relatives from covered walkways, as the monkeys roam freely. Firlands Farmworld is a little further, where you can wander among all sorts of farm animals, as well as a llama or two.

VITAL INFO

CANAL WALK SHOPPING CENTRE 0860 10 1165, daily 10:00–21:00

CHILDREN'S GARDEN AT SPIER 021 809 1159, daily 10:00–17:30

CITY ROCK Observatory, 021 447 1326, Mon–Fri 13:00–21:00, Sat, Sun and holidays 10:00–18:00

MTN SCIENCENTRE Canal Walk, 021 529 8100, Mon–Thurs 9:30–18:00, Fri–Sat 9:30–20:00, Sun 10:00–18:00

RATANGA JUNCTION 086 120 0300 (phone first)

SANCCOB 021 557 6155, feeding times 10:00 and 15:00

THE MAGIC COMPANY 021 534 0244

TYGERBERG ZOO 021 884 4494, daily 9:00, gates close at 17:00 but you can leave later

WEST COAST OSTRICH RANCH 021 972 1955, daily 9:00–17:00

GRANDWEST CASINO

GAMES ARCADE Mon–Thurs 10:00–23:00, Fri & Sat 10:00–01:00, Sun 10:00–23:00

GRANDWEST CASINO & ENTERTAINMENT WORLD Goodwood, 021 505 7777

ICE RINK DAYTIME SESSIONS weekdays 10:00–12:00, 14:00–16:30, Sat 9:00–11:30, 12:00–14:30, 15:00–17:30, Sun 12:00–14:30, 15:00–17:30

MAGIC CASTLE Fri 16:00–24:00, Sat 10:00–24:00, Sun 12:00–20:00, school holidays 12:00–24:00

Outdoor entertainment by the ocean

VITAL INFO

AT THE WATERFRONT

CYBERWORLD 021 419 0156, daily 9:00–21:00

IMAX 021 419 7365, daily 11:30–20:30 (or 21:45 Fri & Sat)

SCRATCH PATCH AND MINERAL WORLD (Also in Simon's Town) 021 419 9429, Mon–Fri 8:30–16:45, Sat, Sun and holidays 9:00–17:30

TELKOM EXPLORATORIUM 021 419 5957, Mon–Sat 9:00–17:00

TWO OCEANS AQUARIUM 021 418 3823, daily 9:30–18:00

SOMERSET WEST

BLUE ROCK CABLE WATERSKI 021 858 1330

FIRLANDS FARMWORLD 021 856 3130, Mon–Fri 8:30–17:00, Sat–Sun 8:30–18:00

MONKEY TOWN 021 858 1060, daily 9:00–17:00

CAPE PENINSULA

CAPE POINT OSTRICH FARM 021 780 9294, daily 9:30–17:30

IMHOFF'S FARM Kommetjie, 021 783 4545, Tues–Sun 10:00–17:00

WORLD OF BIRDS Hout Bay, 021 790 2730, daily 9:00–17:00

The distinctive Namaqualand
daisy in a sea of duiker root

THE ROUTE:
See wild flowers and wild seas all along the Cape's stormy West Coast, from the West Coast National Park to the quaint fishing village of Paternoster.
see MAP A
contact details on pp 146 & 147

TIME: Four days, three nights if you have time on your hands (or one action-packed weekend if work shouts too loudly).

DISTANCE: About 350km (excluding mileage in the West Coast National Park)

BEST TIME TO GO: Spring (August to October) when the wild flowers turn the veld into a rainbow carpet, the whales are frolicking beyond the waves and everything's green after the winter rains. But this is an all-year-round destination, turning sun-bleached and dry in summer, and moody, wild and rugged in winter.

flowers & seas

INTRODUCTION

You'll want to leave your watch behind on any journey up the West Coast, as here time is governed by the sun, the stars and the sea's tides. This coast can be harsh and bleak, with wild seas and hungry rocks gnawing on the skeletons of forsaken ships, but it's also home to millions of the most intricately beautiful wild flowers that dust the veld like a sprinkling of jewels every spring.

You'll meet some unusual, salty characters along the way – these are, after all, the people who gave us bokkems – but they're sunny souls who've tasted sea spray for generations and understand that life should be lived at nature's pace.

This route starts in the Cape Floral Kingdom, smallest but easily the richest of the world's six plant kingdoms, with over 8 600 different species and more than two- thirds found nowhere else in the world.

It then journeys up the West Coast Road into the Cape West Coast Biosphere Reserve, proclaimed by UNESCO in 2000 as an area of exceptional importance, and explores the three major veld types – Strandveld, Sandveld and Renosterveld – with the mighty Atlantic Ocean always at your side.

READING LIST

✓ Be sure to take a good field guide to wild flowers. Try *West Coast – South African Wild Flower Guide* (no. 7), by John Manning and Peter Goldblatt (published by the Botanical Society and the Darling Wild Flower Society, in association with the National Botanical Institute) or the *MTN Flower Watch* by Peter Joyce (Struik).

✓ Take a good bird book, like Kenneth Newman's *Birds of Southern Africa* (Struik).

Floral mosaic

Lambert's Bay

THE ROUTE

Day One
- Breakfast at Blouberg (or visit Groote Post wine estate)
- Veld walk around the Rondeberg Private Nature Reserve
- Picnic in the West Coast National Park
- Overnight in Langebaan

Day Two
- Explore Langebaan or try some action sports
- Lunch at an open-air seafood restaurant
- Watch the sunset from a kayak in the lagoon
- Overnight in Langebaan

Day Three
- Head for Paternoster via the West Coast Fossil Park
- Lunch above the long beach at Paternoster
- Visit Cape Columbine Nature Reserve and South Africa's rudest bay, then take a lighthouse tour
- Overnight in Paternoster

Day Four
- Head for Darling with a stop at the Tienie Versfeld Wildflower Reserve
- Catch a show at Evita se Perron, or lunch at Groote Post
- Sunset and dinner at Blouberg

BEFORE YOU GO
- ✓ Veld walks at Rondeberg Private Nature Reserve need to be booked in advance.
- ✓ The Cape Columbine lighthouse is only open for tours on weekdays.
- ✓ Groote Post wine estate is closed on Sundays.
- ✓ Be sure to book for Tannie Evita's show in Darling. This would mean that you'll miss lunch at Groote Post but you can visit the wine estate on Day One instead.
- ✓ Phone to book ahead for lunch at Die Strandloper restaurant in Langebaan.

flowers & seas

Robben Island with Table Mountain in the background

Make it a weekend!

This route can be completed in one weekend, especially out of flower season. Visit either the West Coast National Park or the Fossil Park on Saturday morning, lunch at Die Strandloper, then overnight in Paternoster. Grab a show in Darling on Sunday and head back for a leisurely dinner in Blouberg. This route can also be done in reverse, as part of the return journey from the Rocks Route (see pp 148–171).

ONE

Waterfront to Blouberg – 30min

Turn left as you leave the Waterfront and follow N1 Paarl. Take second offramp onto R27 (Paarden Eiland, Milnerton). At the traffic lights after 15km turn left into Marine Drive (Blouberg, Atlantic Beach). At 18km turn left into Sir David Baird Drive, then second left into Stadler Road (signed for Café Blouberg). Café Blouberg is at 19km. Ons Huisie is 400m further.

This route starts with a sweep around Table Bay harbour. Interestingly, the bay was first named Saldanha Bay by Portuguese admiral Antonio de Saldanha who anchored here in 1503. The bay was given its new name in 1601, with

today's Saldanha Bay acquiring the admiral's name, even though he in fact never dropped anchor there.

After a rather industrial beginning past the factories of Paarden Eiland you reach Woodbridge Island, which marks the start of the Cape West Coast Biosphere Reserve. Out to sea on your left is Robben Island, most famous as Nelson Mandela's prison for almost two decades. Look back every now and then to see one of the most photographed views in the world – Table Mountain looming majestically out of the sea across Table Bay.

Many photographs are taken from Bloubergstrand (originally Blaauwberg), named after the 231-metre mountain that looks blue from across the bay. It's often windy here, but the kite flyers and

DID YOU KNOW?

As you drive out of Blouberg you'll come to a T-junction of streets named after General Janssens and Sir David Baird, who are still at cross-purposes after almost two centuries. They were the protagonists in the Battle of Blaauwberg in January 1806, which put an end to Dutch rule and marked the start of the second British occupation of the fairest Cape.

133

kitesurfers skimming over the waves make good use of it! There are loads of curios, kites and other goodies for sale along this stretch of Beach Road.

Café Blouberg is *the* breakfast spot. Dating back to 1860, it was once a fisherman's cottage, and some of the original stone walls have been left exposed. Prepare to feast – the menu boasts two and a half pages of breakfast options, including everything from French toast and flapjacks to eggs Florentine. The café is tiny so if it's full keep going to Ons Huisie, another fisherman's cottage which is also a national monument.

Blouberg to Rondeberg – 40min

As you leave Café Blouberg, turn left at the T-junction into Sir David Baird Drive. Go straight through the traffic circle. Turn left at the second circle, then go straight through the third circle. Enter Melkbosstrand (8km). At the traffic lights at about 18km, turn left onto the R27 Velddrif. Turn right into Rondeberg at about 56km.

The road dips into Melkbosstrand before you rejoin the R27. If you're planning a picnic later in the West Coast National Park, turn right towards Cape Town (instead of left to Velddrif) and backtrack a few hundred metres to the Total fuel station and Farmyard Farmstall on your left. It's a mouth-watering pantry of pâtés, preserves, home-baked breads, pies, cakes and quiches. It's pet-friendly too – there're water and dog biscuits at the door.

A little further on look out for the army of power lines marching towards Koeberg nuclear power station on your left. As nuclear power stations go it probably has the best view in the world and must be the only one situated in a nature reserve, surrounded by an abundance of birds and small game.

You'll be tempted to speed up along this stretch of good tar, but keep a sharp eye open for tortoises making their death defying optimistic way across the road, and if you go too fast you'll miss the roadside flowers that spring up from around this point. Also look out for guinea fowl, remembering that if one bursts out of the bushes into the road, there are usually a few more following behind.

On either side of the road you'll see huge amounts of Port Jackson wattle – large bushes with elongated, dark green leaves, which in spring become a riot of fuzzy yellow flowers. These aren't the indigenous flora you came to see, but rather the sad legacy of humans interfering with nature. The early settlers called this area De Groote Woeste Vlakte, or Great Desolate Plain, as its shifting sands and dunes made it almost impassable. In 1845, in an effort to bind and stabilise the sand, Port Jackson wattle and hakea were imported from Australia. These hardy shrubs felt so at home, that they started taking over vast areas of the Cape Flats.

Pass the turning to Groote Post (that's for Day Four, unless you're seeing a show in Darling), then turn into the Rondeberg Private Nature Reserve about 10 kilometres further on for a close look at Sandveld flowers.

At Rondeberg you will receive a huge welcome from Mark and Carol Duckitt, who have converted their dairy farm into a full-time West Coast fynbos reserve. While

MIND THE TORTOISES

Angular, also known as rooi pensie ('red–bellied') tortoises are quite common all over this area. If you see one crossing the road, the kind thing is to stop and move it away from the tar. It's important to put it on the side to which it was heading, otherwise it will simply try to cross the road again. It's a good idea to hold the tortoise well away from your body as you carry it, it will most likely try to pee on your shoes…

both stress that they're not botanists ('we're enthusiastic amateurs'), they have a contagious passion for flowers the rest of us would probably miss. It's taken over four years, but so far they've identified over 800 species on the farm. There's also a dried and pressed specimen of each one in the information centre, along with paintings, life-size watercolours, which were done by their friend and artist Lynda de Wet.

But the idea is to get out and see the real thing, or as Mark puts it: 'Get on your knees, bum in the air and smell them! Get some pollen on your nose. Most people go daisy watching in their cars with air-conditioning and say, "Isn't this lovely!" Well it is, but it's only a tenth of what the West Coast actually has to offer.'

Although the West Coast is famous for the rainbow carpets of daisies in spring, there are flowers to be seen almost every single month of the year.

Mark and Carol take guided walks at 11:00 and 15:00 (but book first), covering about three

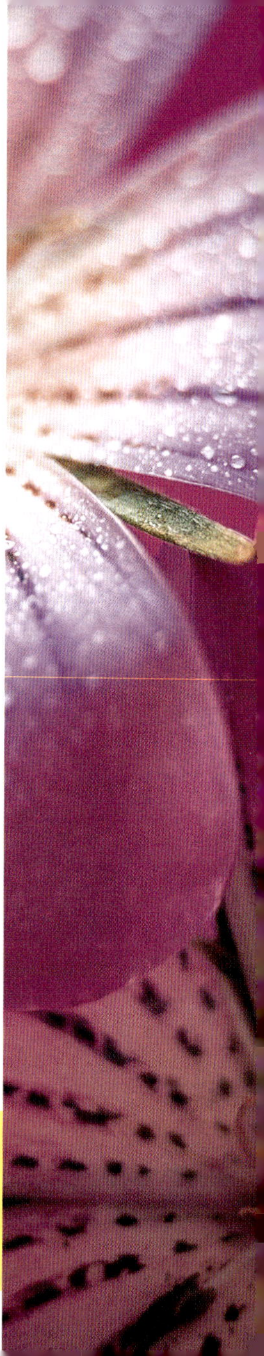

DID YOU KNOW?

There are more plant species in the Cape Peninsula than in the entire United Kingdom.

kilometres in two hours, all on the flat so there's nothing too strenuous. Stay for a lunch of traditional farm-made, West Coast fare (with Mark as wine steward, Carol as waitress and Lynda doing the cooking), or head for the West Coast National Park.

Rondeberg to West Coast National Park – 40min

At the Rondeberg gate, turn right onto the R27. Pass Yzerfontein turn-off after 48km (see detour below). Turn left into West Coast National Park (R27 gate) at 60km.

A little further along the R27 you can take a three-kilometre detour down the Yzerfontein (R315) road to see an old lime kiln, or keep going all the way to Yzerfontein, which is a good place for whale-spotting from June to November.

The West Coast National Park, classified as a wetland of international importance, embraces the majority of the Langebaan lagoon and its islands, attracting an astonishing number of birds. Between 50 000 and 70 000 birds fly a staggering 15 000 kilometres from northern Russia each year to spend their summer around the lagoon. One of the best things about the park is its bird hides, especially the one near the Geelbek visitors' centre. The walkway creeps out into the lagoon, putting you smack in the centre of the avian action. But the park's main claim to fame is the floral kaleidoscope in spring, depending on the rains. Straddling both Strandveld and Sandveld, the land becomes a jewelled carpet of vygies, gazanias, daisies and more.

Peak season is August and September, which is also the only time the Postberg Private Reserve is open. There you can look out for eland, kudu, blue wildebeest, springbok and the stripey Cape mountain zebra. About six kilometres from the main gate the road forks around the lagoon. The Geelbek visitors' centre and restaurant to the right is a good stop for lunch, but otherwise take the left-hand fork down the peninsula. You'll be travelling the right fork later, on your way out of the park to Langebaan. Stop at one of the high points where, on a clear day, you can see all the way to Table Mountain. The road is good tar, becoming gravel near Postberg. Leave the park via the Langebaan gate, which delivers you right into the middle of town. Look back as you climb away from the gate for beautiful views over the lagoon and town.

🔔 **ASK LANGEBAAN TOURISM ABOUT**

✓ Boat trips to the islands in the lagoon, or some way up the Berg River
✓ Scenic tours on off–road motorbikes
✓ Deep–sea game fishing
✓ Scuba diving and wreck diving
✓ Oyster and abalone farming
✓ Buffelsfontein Game Nature Reserve

If all the fresh air is starting to get to you, Langebaan's your town. You can sit at one of the restaurants on the beach, sipping a little chilled chardonnay while the kite- and windsurfers relish the wind, turning the lagoon into a colourful frenzy of soaring sails. When it's calmer the kayakers take to the water, the anglers hit the rocks and playtime begins. The lagoon's water is also marginally warmer than that of the sea, although that's not saying too much as the temperature of the sea is icy cold at the best of times.

Spend the night in Langebaan – there are oceans of guesthouses and B&Bs to choose from. But for something completely different, how about spending a night in a houseboat, bobbing on the lagoon?

Fishing boats on the West Coast

TWO

Day spent in and around Langebaan

This is a deliciously indulgent day. Wander around some of Langebaan's shops, or get energetic at the Cape Sports Center where you can choose from kitesurfing, guided kayaking, windsurfing, mountain biking and dirt bike tours. Or sneak in 18 holes of golf at the Langebaan Country Estate.

Just be back in time to get to the legendary Die Strandloper restaurant by midday. And this is why we love the West Coast – for the beach restaurants where you leave your shoes in the car and can take a dip in the lagoon between courses. No frills here, just excellent food that comes straight from the sea to your tin plate via a sizzle on the open fire. You use a mussel shell as a spoon, and just when you think you can't eat another thing, they slap another seafood delight on the fire. Plenty of potjies filled with treats for the carnivores, along with heavenly fresh oven-baked bread.

An afternoon nap is highly recommended after your lazy lunch. Fit in a sunset kayak on the lagoon if you can, or try your luck at Casino Mykonos.

THREE

Langebaan to West Coast Fossil Park – 15min

From Langebaan Tourism, turn left into Oostewal. After 10km go straight across the R27 to Langebaanweg. At 16.5km turn left at the T-junction onto the R45 Vredenburg. Turn left again into the fossil park at 19.5km.

Leave Langebaan and head inland, through rolling farmlands to the West Coast Fossil Park. Banish any ideas of dry lectures given by dusty academics. This is hands-on stuff, where you can tour the excavation site that's unearthing evidence of African bears, horses with three toes and short-necked giraffes that roamed the coast between two and five million years ago. You can sift for bones yourself, and if you find anything new they'll name it after you. Aim to be there in time for the guided tour and slide show at 11:30.

West Coast Fossil Park to Paternoster – 20min

Leave the fossil park and turn left onto the R45. After 4km, cross the R27 and go straight to Vredenburg. Keep straight at the traffic lights through town, and into Paternoster at 28km.

Heading back towards the sea, the R45 crosses the R27 and takes you to Vredenburg, the thriving commercial centre of this part of the coast. Grab your chance to stock up on supplies – it's a bustling town with supermarkets, chemists, garages and a hospital.

The road through Vredenburg leads directly to Paternoster, one of the most delightful fishing villages along the coast, bravely hanging onto its charm despite the developments happening all around it. Here, in between the cutesy B&Bs, you can still see the

Contrasting splendour

real thing – original white-washed fishing cottages perched on the headland overlooking the long white beach.

Pater noster is Latin for 'Our Father', and the story goes that it was so named after a Portuguese ship wrecked on these treacherous rocks. All the sailors were rescued, and they gave thanks by reciting many a pater noster.

Aim for a lazy lunch at Voorstrandt restaurant, where you'll be tempted to linger over a bottle of wine on the veranda above the sand, until the sun sinks into the sea.

But save some energy for exploring the Cape Columbine Nature Reserve, about five kilometres from Paternoster, which delivers the West Coast at its best – wild seas lashing at a rocky coastline strewn with seashells and seaweed – as well as what has to be South Africa's rudest bay. Follow the signs for Tieties Bay from Die Winkel op Paternoster. The road winds through the original fishing village, and then becomes gravel (a bit rutted) as you approach the reserve. A tour of the lighthouse is also worthwhile, although sadly it's closed on weekends.

Some say that Tieties Bay, at the far end of the Cape Columbine reserve, was named after a fisherman called Titus who drowned there. Others think it refers to the bay's rather well-endowed curve. But the reserve's manager is adamant that it's named after the buxom boulder perched pertly on the hill not far from the lighthouse.

Worth a browse: Die Winkel op Paternoster, near the first stop street as you enter town. Full of ouma's antiques, bric-a-brac and delicious preserves.

• Paternoster se Padstal, on the right just before the hotel, has

every kind of pickled fish, preserve and even rose jam – once you get past the bokkems at the entrance.

- Die Pomphuis Gallery near Voorstrandt restaurant.
- The shops at the fish market.

FOUR

Paternoster to Darling – 1hr

From Die Winkel op Paternoster, return through Vredenburg to R27 (24km) and turn right to Cape Town. At 72km, turn left onto R315 Darling. Tienie Versfeld Wildflower Reserve is on the right at 75km. Enter Darling at 86km. Turn left into Hoof Street, second left into Kerk Street, then second right into Arcadia Street. Evita se Perron is on the left at about 87km.

Heading for home you can either retrace your route through Vredenburg and onto the R27, or take a longer route via St Helena Bay (take the gravel road signposted Stompneusbaai as you leave Paternoster – ask a local about the road's condition before you set off). St Helena Bay is slightly more industrial than scenic – it has one of the biggest fish canning factories in the southern hemisphere – but it's also the place where Portuguese explorer Vasco da Gama first touched southern African soil on 7 November 1497. A cross marks the spot. The village's other claim to fame is that it's the only place on the West Coast where you can watch the sun rise over the sea, due to its position on the bay.

You'll stumble over the Tienie Versfeld Wildflower Reserve about three kilometres after you turn off the R27. Entrance is free and the gates are always open – actually there is no gate, just a wooden stile to climb over the fence. This is pristine Renosterveld and there are at least two flowers, the yellow wine cup and the red-flowered sundew, that are found only in the reserve. Renosterveld is very scarce – less than four percent of its original extent still exists. Tienie Versfeld safeguarded these 20 hectares when he donated part of his farm to the National Botanical Institute in 1958. He is now buried in the reserve, amid the rich diversity of blooms he helped protect.

Darling is home to South Africa's most famous satirist, Pieter-Dirk Uys (aka Evita Bezuidenhout), whose state of the nation

GOOD TO KNOW

The Hello Darling Arts Festival normally takes place during September, coinciding with the Darling Wildflower Show that has been held almost every year in September since 1917.

revues at Evita se Perron – the old Darling railway station – keep a humorously sharp eye on our fledgeling democracy with a wit that cuts to the bone.

Enjoy an afternoon or evening show over a plate of traditional *boerekos*, washed down with lashings of satire, sit outdoors on the Piazza dolcEvita or browse around Evita se A en C, the arts and crafts shop full of soaps, candles and other gifty goodies made in the area, as well as a collection of Africana books.

Darling to Groote Post – 30min

When you leave Evita se Perron, turn left and left again into Hoof Street, heading out of town. After 10km, turn right onto gravel, signed to Groote Post. Turn left into Groote Post at 18km. (If going straight to Cape Town, stay on the tar past the turn-off to Groote Post. At 20km, turn right R307 (R27) Cape Town. At 33km turn left onto R27 Cape Town.)

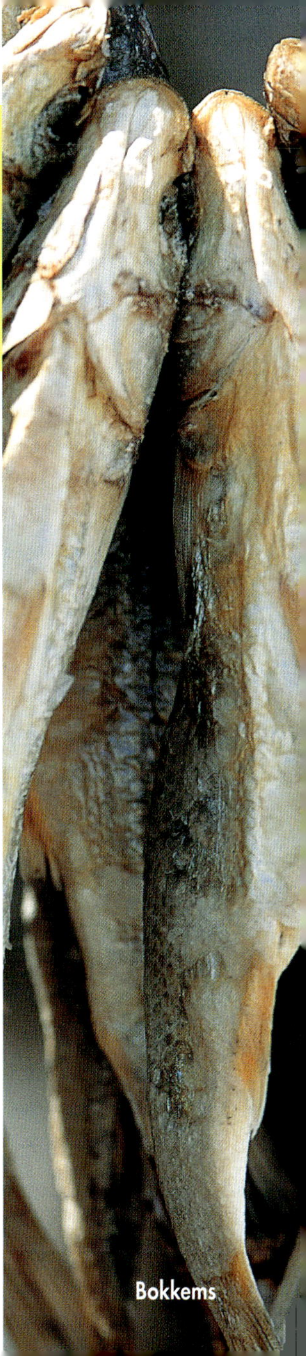

Bokkems

Head out of Darling on Hoof Street and you'll see a signposted turn-off to Groote Post wine estate after about 10 kilometres. Be prepared for about another 10 kilometres on gravel – it's a good idea to phone Groote Post to check the road's condition, especially if there's been a lot of rain.

Groote Post, a national monument, is a gorgeous farm dating way back to 1706 that now focuses on producing a range of excellent red and white wines. Taste them all in the winery (once an eighteenth-century fort), and then settle back for a delectable lunch in the high-ceilinged, yellowwood-floored manor house.

Groote Post to Blouberg – 45min

Turn left onto main gravel road. After 10km, turn left on R27. At about 50km, at traffic lights turn right into Blaauwberg Road M14. At 1km, T-junction right into Beach Road (Marine Drive). At 53km turn left into Sir David Baird then second left into Stadler. On the Rocks is at about 54km.

It's an easy drive to the last stop on this route, On the Rocks restaurant in Bloubergstrand, from where you can watch the sun set over the sea as Table Mountain turns from green to purple. From there retrace the route you took on Day One back to the Waterfront on the R27 and the N1.

ARE THE FLOWERS AS GOOD AS THEY USED TO BE?

Well, it depends what you're looking for. Hannes Kleynhans, a conservationist who runs the Beach Camp in Cape Columbine Nature Reserve, gives some challenging insights:

'Those blankets of daisies you see in pictures only grow on land that's been ploughed or churned up at the roadsides, because they're actually weeds. The real beauty of the West Coast is its incredible diversity, and now that more land is being set aside for conservation, that diversity is coming back. So yes, the flowers are getting better, even if there are fewer daisies. But of course you can't see that at 150 kilometres an hour – you need to get out and walk.'

Namaqualand in spring

VITAL INFO

CAFÉ BLOUBERG Blouberg, 021 554 4462, open daily 9:00–22:00

CAPE COLUMBINE LIGHTHOUSE 021 449 2400, open weekdays 10:00–15:00, closed weekends

CAPE COLUMBINE NATURE RESERVE 5km from Paternoster, 022 752 2718, day visitors 7:00–19:00

CAPE SPORTS CENTER 022 772 1114, www.capesport.co.za

CASINO MYKONOS Club Mykonos, Langebaan, 022 707 6970

DIE POMPHUIS GALLERY 022 752 2058, daily 10:00–17:00 or so, depending on the weather

DIE STRANDLOPER Langebaan, 022 772 2490 or 083 227 7195, lunch and dinner daily in season, otherwise depending on bookings, booking essential

DIE WINKEL OP PATERNOSTER 022 752 2632, daily 10:00–16:30

EVITA SE PERRON Old Darling railway station, 022 492 2831

GROOTE POST WINE ESTATE 022 492 2825, wine tastings Mon–Fri 9:00–17:00, Sat 9:00–15:00, closed Sun, restaurant: lunches only

LANGEBAAN COUNTRY ESTATE 022 772 2112

ONS HUISIE Blouberg, 021 554 1553, open daily 9:00–22:00

PATERNOSTER SE PADSTAL 084 762 5656, daily 9:00–17:30

RONDEBERG PRIVATE NATURE RESERVE 022 492 3099, www.rondeberg.co.za, open Easter to Christmas, booking essential

VOORSTRANDT RESTAURANT 022 752 2038, open daily 10:00–22:00

WEST COAST FOSSIL PARK 022 766 1606, open weekdays 8:00–16:00, Sat–Sun 9:00–13:00

WEST COAST NATIONAL PARK AND POSTBERG RESERVE 022 772 2144, main gates open daily 7:00–19:00, Postberg normally open Aug & Sept only, 8:00–17:00

Circling seagulls await their dinner

VITAL INFO

REGIONAL TOURISM BUREAUS

DARLING TOURISM BUREAU, cnr Pastorie & Hill streets. 022 492 3361, darlinginfo@mweb.co.za

LANGEBAAN TOURISM BUREAU, Bree Street, 022 772 1515, lbninfo@mweb.co.za, www.langebaaninfo.com

WEST COAST PENINSULA TOURISM BUREAU (Paternoster/Vredenburg/ St Helena Bay), 022 715 1142, tour@mailbox.co.za

WEST COAST REGIONAL TOURISM Organisation Moorreesburg, 022 433 2380, tourism@capewestcoast.org, www.capewestcoast.org

WHERE TO STAY:

LANGEBAAN

HOUSEBOATS ON LANGEBAAN LAGOON private operator: 022 492 3944 or 082 882 9001, SA National Parks boat: 021 552 0008

THE FARMHOUSE HOTEL 5 Egret Street, 022 772 2062, www.thefarmhouselangebaan.co.za

PATERNOSTER

THE BEACH CAMP, CAPE COLUMBINE NATURE RESERVE Paternoster, 082 926 2267, info@ratrace.co.za, www.ratrace.co.za

THE OYSTERCATCHER'S HAVEN 48 Sonkwas Way, Paternoster, on the edge of the Cape Columbine Reserve, 022 752 2193, info@oystercatchershaven.com, www.oystercatchershaven.com

Sandstone rocks naturally sculpted by the sea

THE ROUTE:

Let the Cape rock you as you climb monster boulders in Paarl, then explore the Cederberg's ancient rock art and wild mountain formations.

see MAP A,
contact details on pp 170 & 171

TIME: Two nights, three days. But if you have more time, take a fourth day in the Cederberg, overnighting at Sanddrif or Kromrivier.

DISTANCE: About 500km, ending in Clanwilliam. Add 240km for the direct route back to Cape Town on the N7, or 170km to join the Flowers & Seas Route via Lambert's Bay.

BEST TIME TO GO: All year, although spring and autumn are best – the weather is warm but still mild. Be prepared for temperatures over 30 °C in summer. Winter's cooler weather is good for hiking, but rain and snow can make the gravel roads more treacherous.

rocks

INTRODUCTION

This is a route of wild rocks and towering mountain passes – arguably the most dramatic and scenic route in this book. You'll see some most astonishing rock formations, forged out of ancient cataclysmic events, then delicately decorated by the San who roamed these mountains hundreds and thousands of years ago.

The route starts with a walk up the mother of all rocks, a huge colossus of granite above Paarl, then journeys through the Cederberg to Agter Pakhuis in an area that may have more rock paintings per square kilometre than anywhere else in southern Africa.

These are the roads less travelled, beautiful drives through remote and rugged rockscapes and endless valley vistas. The solitude means the nights sparkle with thousands of stars, which the Bushmen believed were embers drifting up from the night fires to dance in the heavens. We'll never unravel the mysteries of the Bushmen, but we can guess at their spirit through the art they left behind.

READING LIST

✓ Don't go without Peter Slingsby's *Cederberg: The Map* (Baardskeerder), and his books on rock art sites. Look out for *Rock Art of the Western Cape: Book 1: Traveller's Rest and the Sevilla Trail*; *Book 2: Bushmans Kloof*; *Book 3: Cederberg Conservancy and Eastern Koue Bokkeveld* (all The Fontmaker).

✓ Another book to pack is *Some Views on Rock Paintings in the Cederberg*, by Janette Deacon.

✓ Take *Wild Flower Guide number 10: Cederberg* (Botanical Society), to identify the flora.

✓ *The Romance of Cape Town Passes*, by Graham Ross (David Philip) gives you all the historical background.

Quartz crystals

Bain's Kloof Pass

THE ROUTE

Day One
- Walk to the top of Paarl Rock
- Drive Bain's Kloof to Ceres (pack a picnic)
- Explore the rock art near Op-die-Berg
- Overnight at Mount Ceder or Kagga Kamma

Day Two
- Discover Stadsaal and Truitjieskraal in the Cederberg
- Taste Cederberg wine and swim at Maalgat
- Overnight near Clanwilliam

Day Three
- View rock art on the Sevilla and Salmanslaagte trails
- Lunch at the mission station of Wupperthal before touring the famous shoe factory
- Head back to Cape Town, or
- Go on to Lambert's Bay on the coast via the Heerenlogement Cave to join the Flowers & Seas Route back to Cape Town

Note: Fuel is not readily available in the Cederberg, so be sure to fill up in Paarl, Wellington, Ceres, Op-die-Berg (8:00–17:00), Citrusdal or Clanwilliam.

BEFORE YOU GO

- ✓ This entire route is suitable for a saloon car (unless there's been some extreme bad weather), but a 4x4 would be more comfortable. Phone ahead to check the condition of the roads in winter.

- ✓ Cellphone reception is patchy or non-existent on this route, particularly after Day One.

- ✓ The Sevilla rock art trail near Clanwilliam is tough in summer's heat, especially November to February. If you do it then, aim to start walking early – even at 5:00 – so you can be out of the sun by 9:00.

- ✓ If you're travelling in a tall camper or bus, make sure that you can pass under 3.8m – the height of an overhanging rock on Bain's Kloof.

De Hangen
Pakhuis Conservancy
Salmanslaagte
R364
TO THE NORTHERN CAPE
Traveller's Rest
Englishman's Grave
TO KLAWER
Mount Synott 698m
Suurkop 650m
PAKHUISBERG
Muurkraal
Leipoldt's Grave
Sevilla Trail
Bushman's Kloof
R364
Pakhuis Pass
Clanwilliam
Osberg 941m
Agterfontein
TO LAMBERT'S BAY
Heuningvlei
Tra-Tra Mountains
Cederberg Wilderness Area
Die Hoekie
Wupperthal Conservancy
CEDERBERG
N7
Wupperthal
Warmhoekkop 1 127m
Middelberg North 1 516m
Sneeukop 1 930m
Algeria
Vaaldam
Tafelberg 1 969m
Wolfberg Arch
Uitkyk Pass
Perdewater
Wolfberg 1 609m
Voëlfontein
Wolfberg Cracks
N7
Maltese Cross
Matjiesrivier Nature Reserve
Sneeuberg 2 027m
Dwarsrivier
Cederberg Tourist Park
Stadsaal
Kromrivier
Donkerkloofkop 1 746m
Truitjieskraal
Klipbokberg 1 391m
Citrusdal
Grootrivier Pass
MIDDELBERG
Varkkloof
TO ELAND'S BAY
R365
Middelberg Peak 1 565m
Grootberg 1 356m
R303
TO KAGGA KAMMA
N7
TO PIKETBERG
Heksrivier
TO CERES

Heerenlogement Cave
Pakhuis Pass
Lambert's Bay
Graafwate
Clanwilliam
Eland's Bay
Wupperthal
Cederberg
Citrusdal
N7
Kagga Kamma
Vredenburg
Piketberg
N7
Great Winterhoek Wilderness Area
Op-die-Berg
N1
Ceres
Malmesbury
Bain's Pass
N7
Wellington
Paarl
N1
Milnerton
CAPE TOWN
N2

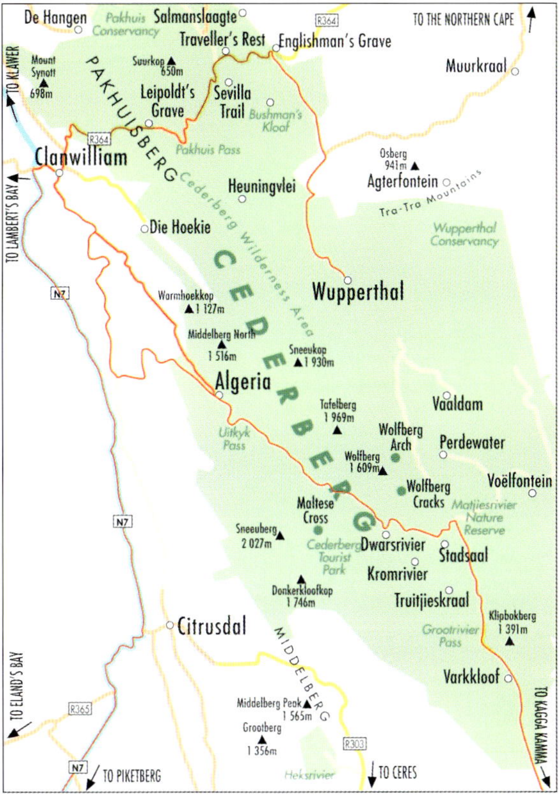

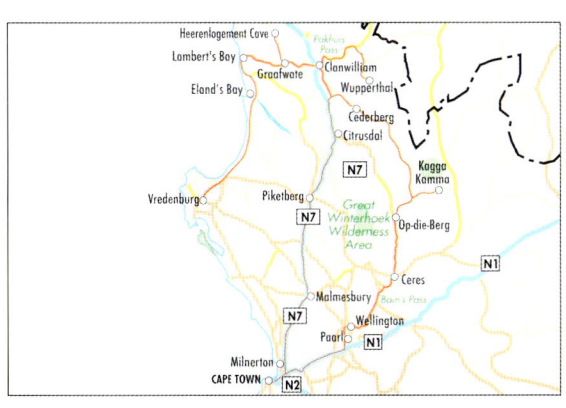

View from Paarl Rock

ONE

Waterfront to Paarl Rocks – 1hr 10min

From the Waterfront, turn left and follow signs to N1 Paarl. Around
53km take Exit 55, R45 (R101) Paarl Main Road and Franschhoek
and turn left at the stop. At 55km turn left on to Jan Phillips Drive,
signed Paarl Mountain Reserve (becomes gravel). At 57km
T-junction right to Paarl Mountain Reserve. Pass a picnic area and
toilets at 61km – keep right to the rocks. 400m later keep left to
rocks, through the boom at 62km. Park after 500m and take an
easy walk onto the top of Paarl Rock, but for more impressive rocks
drive another 500m.

At 48 kilometres you'll see some rather phallic, swooping white
stone columns up on a hill on the left. That's the Taal (Language)
Monument, inaugurated in 1975 to commemorate the origin and
growth of Afrikaans.

A colossal cluster of granite domes that soar 654 metres into the sky sets the tone for this rocky route, named the Paarl ('Pearl') mountains by the very first European visitors because of the way they glisten when it rains. (The local Khoikhoi called them the Tortoise mountains.) Paarl Rock, which dominates the town below, is the first boulder you come to – on top is an old cannon that used to be fired to tell local farmers a ship needing fresh produce had come into Table Bay – but keep going to the more impressive Britannia (on the left) and Gordon's rocks further up the road. There's an easy path

HAUNTED ROCK

They say the ghost of a murderer still haunts the hollowed-out boulder on top of Paarl Rock that he used as a hideaway. Smoke from his fire gave him away and he was hanged, but wisps can sometimes still be seen at dawn...

to the top of Britannia Rock, from where you can see all the way to Table Mountain, with absolutely breathtaking 360-degree views of the Paarl Valley and the Peninsula. Although the path up is steep, with chains to help over the awkward bits, it's worth it. If you're reasonably fit you'll do it in 10 minutes, the rest of us need 15 or 20. Once back in the car, note that the drive down follows a different route to the way up!

Paarl Rocks to Op-die-Berg via Ceres and Prince Alfred Hamlet – 2hr 15min (excluding time for lunch)

From the top parking area, follow the road down and through boom. At 2.8km, turn left – this is not signposted. At the stop (8km) turn left, then right to the R45 to Wellington, Malmesbury. At 13km turn right at the four-way stop to R44 Wellington. (Ignore next left to Hermon, Ceres.) At the traffic lights and T-junction at about 18km, turn left to Wellington. At the church, turn right at the traffic lights to Wolseley, Ceres via Bain's Kloof. Bain's Kloof village is at the top of the pass at about 34km. Ignore the right turn to Worcester at about 49km and go straight to Wolseley, Ceres. (Ignore next left to Wolseley.) At 63km, cross the Breede River and at the T-junction turn right to R46 Ceres and cross Michell's Pass. Enter Ceres. At about 73km, turn left at the lights to R303 PA Hamlet, Op-die-Berg and Citrusdal. You'll pass through Prince Alfred Hamlet at about 81km, and start the Gydo Pass. (Ignore right to Touws River.) At 115km, turn left into Op-die-Berg.

Ceres as seen from the Gydo Pass

The road almost all the way from Ceres is flanked by two starkly different mountain ranges. The Swartruggens mountains rise serenely on the right, while on the left, the tormented rocks of the Witsenberg and Skurweberg ('Scaly Mountains') lie scattered and shattered, victims of some horrendous cataclysm that must have rocked the earth here.

Op-die-Berg ('On the Mountain') is a tiny hamlet that's home to Wethu Experiences, a community-based project that brings much needed tourism to the area. They will take you on an interesting two and a half hour rock art tour to three ancient sites, starting with an open living area, then a birthing site, and lastly through a 10 metre high tunnel to a fascinating shaman site. (This can be combined with a kid and granny-friendly donkey cart excursion.) Wethu also offers mountain bike rides

and hiking in the Skurweberg and the Swartruggens Nature Conservancy, which might be under snow around August and September. Booking for the Wethu tour is essential.

The rock art site is en route to the overnight stops at Kagga Kamma or Mount Ceder. If you'd like to go on from the site (instead of returning to Op-die-Berg with the guide), let them know in advance.

It's not far to the two overnight spots – Mount Ceder's cottages on the river or Kagga Kamma, which is priced for the international market. Alternatives are Klein Cederberg (stone cabins, with rock art sites), Zoo Ridge guesthouse, Nuwerust (self-catering) and Rietvlei (B&B).

Op-die Berg to Mount Ceder – 45min

Turn back onto the R303. After 500m, turn right onto R355 Ceres–Karoo and Cederberg. The tar ends at about 17km – keep straight to Cederberg (or turn right here to Kagga Kamma). After the Blinkberg Pass turn right into Mount Ceder at 51km.

Mount Ceder has several tastefully decorated stone cottages, four of which are on a perennial river – enjoy a quick dip and sundowner amid the tranquillity. Ask about their hiking routes and rock art site – a short drive, then a 10-minute walk. Horse trails (one to three hours) can be arranged. (Self-catering, licensed restaurant.)

Or go to Kagga Kamma
(1hr 5min from Op-die-Berg)

Turn right at 17km (see above). After Katbakkies Pass turn left at 37km to Kagga Kamma.

The lodge at the 15 000-hectare Kagga Kamma Private Game Reserve is set among boulders and weathered stones which hide a number of rock art sites. Get there in time for sundowners over the canyon, then go for a night game drive and enjoy the stars. In the morning, join a guided tour of the San art – the cheetah paintings here are the only ones found in South Africa. Accommodation is in luxury thatched huts or 'cave suites' tucked among the boulders (full board).

TWO

This is a fairly packed day – to make all the stops, be on the road by 8:00 and if you use the suggested times at each place as a guide, you'll be at Traveller's Rest by about 17:30. Otherwise skip one or two of the stops.

(If you stayed at Kagga Kamma, you have further to drive and definitely won't be able to make all these stops, but there is the benefit of a morning rock art tour at Kagga Kamma.)

Mount Ceder to Stadsaal – 40min (excluding stop for permits)

Turn out of Mount Ceder towards Cederberg. At 11km turn left to Clanwilliam, and left again at 19km (Matjiesrivier Nature Reserve office is on your left). Turn left to Stadsaal Cave and Bushmen paintings at about 22km. Allow about 45min at Stadsaal.

Stadsaal is a weird honeycomb of rocks weathered into astonishing shapes, the centrepiece being the imposing Stadsaal Cave. Translated as 'Town Hall Cave', Stadsaal was a gathering place for farmers in the district, and politicians like DF Malan – also known as the architect of apartheid – would address his constituents there. His signature is one of many on the rocks. Also look out for C Louis Leipoldt's, as well as PW Botha's, although his has become somewhat pockmarked.

The rock art is not far from the gate along a track to the right before you get

The Wolfberg Cracks

TREAD LIGHTLY AND TAKE CARE

This legacy of rock art is priceless and vulnerable. Many sites have been defaced or damaged, so take special care:

- ✓ Don't touch the paintings – the smallest amount of moisture on your fingers causes damaging salts to accumulate on the rock surface.
- ✓ Don't even think of wetting them – salts will be drawn to the surface where they expand and destroy the painting.
- ✓ Don't make fires or stir up dust.
- ✓ Be careful not to brush the paintings with your clothing, rucksack or camera bag.
- ✓ It's an offence in terms of the National Heritage Resources Act (Act 25 of 1999) to damage, destroy or alter rock paintings. The penalty is a fine up to R100 000 or five years in jail.

(From Dr Janette Deacon, Heritage Western Cape and the SA Heritage Resources Agency (SAHRA, formerly National Monuments Council).

160

Interesting rock formations in the Cederberg

to Stadsaal. Although they may be two or three thousand years old, these elephants are beautifully preserved. No figure is armed, so this probably doesn't represent a hunt, and it's unusual in that this wouldn't have been a living area, so who knows why the artist chose to paint here?

Permits (and a key) are required for Stadsaal and the Bushman paintings, available at Matjiesrivier Nature Reserve office, Kromrivier and Dwarsrivier, and Algeria. Kromrivier issues permits for Truitjieskraal. Dwarsrivier issues permits for Maalgat (as well as Wolfberg Cracks, Lot's Wife and the Maltese Cross, if you're making this a longer stay).

Stadsaal to Kromrivier – 20min

Turn back onto the main road, then left to Kromrivier after about 3km. Allow 1.5hr including drive to Truitjieskraal.

The road drops quite sharply down to Kromrivier farm, where you'll meet the first of the Nieuwoudt families who pop up all through this valley. Get a permit at the office, then drive roughly four kilometres through the farm (closing gates behind you) to Truitjieskraal, a mysterious world of unusually eerie quiet.

Take time to wander about this huge massif of sculpted rocks, weathered slabs, stacks, towers and sentinels. In between are two rock art sites with interesting trance images, and an extremely rare half-man half-animal figure. The mummified remains of a San baby were found here several years ago.

A river runs through Kromrivier ('Crooked River'), with basic chalets and campsites on the river banks. Horse rides are available, and there's a restaurant, so this makes a good spot for lunch. If you're staying longer, there are several beautiful hikes to waterfalls and rock pools as well as a 4x4 trail. Ask about more rock art at Potation, and Kippurs and Kromrivier caves.

Kromrivier to Dwarsrivier – 20min

Return to main road and turn left to Clanwilliam. Turn left to the Dwarsrivier office after about 3km. Allow 45min for a wine tasting and at least 1.5hr for the walk and swim at Maalgat.

Look up and to your right as you approach Sanddrif and Dwarsrivier at one of the Cederberg's famous formations, the Wolfberg Cracks, which disappear into the rock face right at

12 PASSES

On this route you'll drive all these passes (and some of them twice):
Bain's Kloof, Michell's, Gydo, Blinkberg, Grootrivier, Uitkyk, Pakhuis, Hoek se Berg, Kouberg, Katbakkies, Nieuwoudt and Piekenierskloof passes, the last three depending on the route you choose to take.

the top of the mountain, and the army of extraordinary rock sentinels on your right. Turn in at Dwarsrivier farm (owned by more Nieuwoudts) and visit the Cederberg Private Cellar to taste 'wines with altitude' – this is South Africa's highest winery, at over a thousand metres above sea level. They make a range of red and white wines which, as they say, will rock you. (Closed on Sundays.)

Now, fancy a swim in one of the most fantastic rock pools in the Western Cape? It's a short drive and then an easy, mostly level 25-minute walk to Maalgat ('Whirlpool'), a 'bottomless' pool fed by a gushing waterfall, with awesomely high rock diving boards for those who need to prove something. Get directions and a permit from the Dwarsrivier office. Dwarsrivier has camping and chalets on the lawns on either side of the river at Sanddrif. An observatory operates on Saturday nights except at full moon – ask at the office.

Dwarsrivier to Algeria – 35min

Leave Dwarsrivier and continue on the road. After Uitkyk (Lookout) Pass, turn right to Algeria Forest Station at about 26km. This is an optional stop, but the office (and you'll probably find yet another Nieuwoudt behind the desk) has a very good information centre and a relief model of the entire area which helps give you the big picture of these mountain ranges.

A two and a half hour walk to a waterfall starts here, as well as numerous longer hikes. Algeria also has a beautifully lawned campsite and several stone cottages for hire. (The Algeria

Forestry Station was so named because it reminded the first forester, George Bath, of the Atlas mountains in North Africa.)

Algeria to Traveller's Rest
via Clanwilliam – 1hr 10min

Leave Algeria. After 400m turn right to Clanwilliam. At the T-junction at 22km, turn right to Clanwilliam. Keep straight through town. At the T-junction turn right onto R364 Wupperthal, Calvinia. At 46km stop at the grave of C Louis Leipoldt. Climb Pakhuis (Warehouse) Pass, cross the Brandewyn (Brandy) River at 63km and turn left to Traveller's Rest 300m later.

(An alternative, slower route to Clanwilliam traces the edge of the dam and then joins the above road – it's scenic except at the end of summer when the water is low. You could also access Clanwilliam on the N7, although this is a narrow road with lots of truck traffic to slow you down.)

The otherworldly rock formations around the Pakhuis Pass set the scene for Traveller's Rest, the kick-off place for two of the best rock art galleries in this area – the Sevilla Trail and Salmanslaagte, which can be visited on Day Three (remember to get your permits here).

The appeal at Traveller's Rest is the rock art rather than the accommodation, which is rustic with 'a good bed and clean bathroom,' says owner Haffie Strauss. 'After all, the whole idea is to get away!' There are 12 basic cottages scattered around the area. The Khoisan Kitchen restaurant is open by appointment, and full-time during August and September. (All the cottages have huge fireplaces for winter.)

For more creature comforts contact Clanwilliam Tourism for guesthouses in the town, or for out of this world luxury (and prices to match), go to the Bushmans Kloof Wilderness Reserve, a Relais & Chateau lodge. It's a green oasis in a parched and rugged area, with beautiful lawns, several swimming pools, a most heavenly spa, delicious food (mainly eaten al fresco) and fabulously luxurious suites.

The lodge is set among fantastic rock formations, and there are over 130 rock art sites, making it one of the most densely painted areas in the country. Your stay will include game drives

Bushmen or San?

There aren't any universally accepted terms, but your safest bet is with San and Khoisan. The former would indicate the Bushman hunter-gatherers, while Khoisan is a word to describe both the San and Khoekhoen pastoralists. Some descendants in Namibia and Botswana prefer to call themselves Bushmen. The term Hottentot has largely unflattering origins and is unacceptable today.

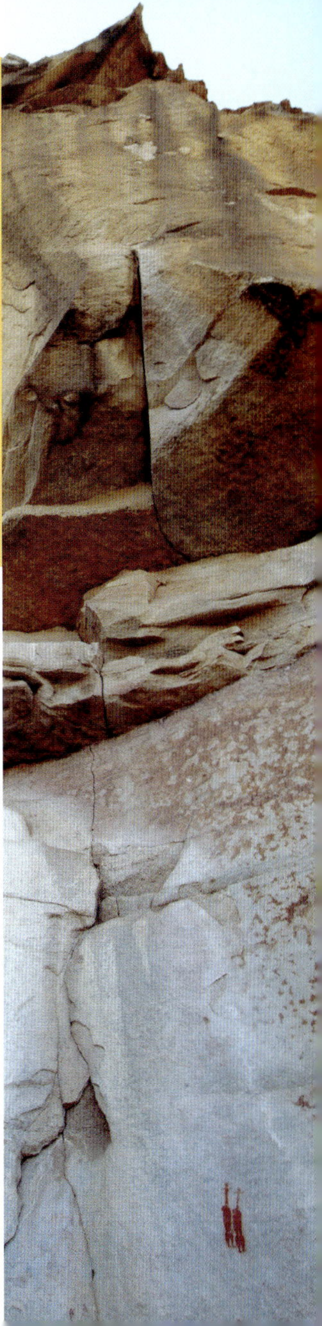

and tours of some of the rock art sites, with informed guides who can give some of the background to the paintings. You can also take a garden tour, go mountain biking, canoeing, fishing or try your hand at some abseiling and rock climbing.

About a kilometre and a half past Traveller's Rest, turn right into the grand entrance of Bushmans Kloof. The lodge is just over seven kilometres further.

THREE

The Sevilla Trail is a great four kilometre ramble, marked by white footprints, through the world of the San to 10 sites scattered below high cliffs, among boulders and on rocky ledges. It takes about two and a half to three hours, and should be done in the early morning in summer – aim to be back and out of the sun by 9:00 or you may find the heat unbearable.

The paintings may be 1 600–2 000 years old, although they could go back 8 000 years, and include some fantastical figures of monsters, a remarkable group of dancing ladies, handprints, and an extremely unusual 'face' overlayed with a pattern of geometric lines. Site 10 is across the river – don't cross if it's swollen with winter rains, rather retrace your steps.

Salmanslaagte is a six kilometre circular walk (or you can get almost all the way to it in a 4x4) to caves with three sites, named after Salman ('Soloman'), a shepherd who lived here. One of the first paintings you see is of three women showing the remarkable San steatopygia, the enormous buttocks, which allowed them to store fatty reserves of food.

Also of interest are the huge yellow elephants – one is about one and a half square metres – which must have required a large amount of yellow ochre that is not found in the Traveller's Rest area. (And just in case we think we've solved the mysteries of the San, there's a painting that looks very similar to a Persian carpet. You figure it out.)

Traveller's Rest to Wupperthal – 45min

Start at Traveller's Rest and turn left onto the R364 (away from Clanwilliam). At 5.3km turn right at the grave to Biedouw Valley and Wupperthal. Go over Hoek se Berg Pass, past the Biedouw Valley and down the Kouberg Pass into Wupperthal at 36km.

After the morning's walks (and a breather), head to the Moravian Mission town of Wupperthal for

WHO WAS C LOUIS LEIPOLDT?

His lonely grave is on the R364 Wupperthal, Calvinia, under an overhang that has some rock art on it. He was a renowned Afrikaans poet, and practised as a physician in Clanwilliam. He was also the grandson of one of the missionaries who founded Wupperthal.

lunch (phone the tourism bureau to book) and a gentle exploration of this tiny hamlet on the banks of the Tra-Tra River ('tra-tra' is a Khoisan name meaning 'bushy'). Started in 1830 by two German Rhenish missionaries, who were reminded of the Wupper Valley at home, it was taken over by the Moravian missionaries in 1965.

Today it's famous for its veldskoene (bush shoes – you can tour the factory) and rooibos ('red bush') tea – a caffeine-free, low tannin tea with health-giving properties, made from a plant that grows only in the Cederberg mountain area.

The road turns down to Wupperthal at the lonely Engelsman se Graf ('Englishman's Grave'), where infantryman Lt Graham Clowes fell during a skirmish with Boer soldiers in the South African (Anglo-Boer) War.

After Wupperthal, return to Cape Town on the N7, or extend your trip by joining up with the Flowers & Seas Route (see pp 126–147) on the West Coast, via the historic Heerenlogement Cave ('Gentlemen's Lodging') and Lambert's Bay's Bird Island and open-air restaurants.

Clanwilliam to Cape Town on the N7 – 2hr 40min

Return to Clanwilliam, keep straight through town. Turn left to N7 Citrusdal, Klawer, then left to N7 Citrusdal. After about 57km you'll be on top of the Piekenierskloof Pass. Follow the N7 to Cape Town until about 210km, when you'll cross over the N1 highway. Take Exit 13, which loops round to join the N1 Cape Town. Enter the city and follow Waterfront signs at about 240km

Clanwilliam to Lambert's Bay – 35 min

Keep straight through town, ignore left to N7 Citrusdal, Klawer. You'll enter Lambert's Bay at about 57km. (Detour to Heerenlogement Cave is an extra 28km.)

The Heerenlogement Cave is at about 28 kilometres from Clanwilliam. Cross the bridge and turn right to Graafwater. You'll see a sign for the Heerenlogement at about 51 kilometres.

The cave was used as a 'gentlemen's lodging' by travellers as early as Governor Simon van der Stel, who signed his name while en route to investigate the feasibility of copper mining in Namaqualand in 1685. There are mentions of the cave and a tree growing from a cleft in the rock roof in journals as far back as 1712 – the tree is still there and looking very strong!

If you're in a 4x4 you can try some seriously fun sand driving at The Dunes in Lambert's Bay, but the town's main claim to fame is Bird Island, a three-hectare slab of rock that's home to about 14 000 Cape gannets and is the world's only gannet breeding colony that's accessible on foot – it's just a short walk along the harbour wall.

The island also hosts large numbers of cormorants and penguins, and judging by the decibel level, they're all shouting at each other. But suffer the noise, because the sight of several thousand densely packed and squabbling gannets is unforgettable, as is the smell.

There are also two of the West Coast's famous open-air restaurants just outside Lambert's Bay: Bosduifklip, set in a rocky amphitheatre on the way into town, and Muisbosskerm, on the beach on the road down to Elands Bay. Allow several hours to indulge in course after course of food cooked on the fire.

If all this requires an overnight stop, call Lambert's Bay Tourism for accommodation options. Then head for Velddrif, where you can decide where to pick up the Flowers & Seas Route.

Lambert's Bay to Velddrif – 1hr

Part of the road requires a permit – buy one at the BP garage in the main street, or at the toll booth for a little extra. Zero odometer at Lambert's Bay. At 9.5km veer right to toll road (toll booth is at 13km). At Eland's Bay (24km), T-junction left then 1km later, oblique T-junction right to R366 Aurora, Dwarskersbos and Velddrif. About 300m later, turn again to R27 Aurora, Dwarskersbos and Velddrif. At about 59km, turn right to Velddrif and Dwarskersbos – this is very easy to miss! At 90km drive through Velddrif. Either turn right after the town for Vredenburg and Paternoster, or remain on R27 past Langebaan to the West Coast National Park.

Velddrif to Cape Town – 3hr

Stay on the R27 and follow the signs back to Cape Town.

ROCK PAINTINGS

Who were the artists? The paintings are generally attributed to the San people (or Bushmen), Stone Age hunter-gatherers who later came into contact with the Khoekhoen, or Hottentot herders and pastoralists. Together they are sometimes called the Khoisan.

When were the paintings created? It is unfortunately impossible to carbon date the paintings without destroying them, and science is also unable to date reliably the ochre paint most commonly used. Cave litter places the inhabitants as far back as 100 000 years, although the first painters were probably active 8 000 years ago. Scenes of Europeans tell us the San were still painting here within the last 350 years.

What did they depict? Without asking the artists it's hard to know for sure. While some paintings seem to illustrate what they saw every day, it's almost certain that most were deeply spiritual, reflecting their reverence for nature and quest for supernatural power and inspiration. Much is the creation of shamans, or medicine people, who painted their trance or dream-state experiences.

What materials were used? Clay, red and yellow ochre and charcoal were ground into a fine powder and mixed with water, blood, egg or plant juices.

Why are some unfinished? Often the artwork appears incomplete. The explanation is that red ochre bonded well with the rock canvas, lasting thousands of years, while black, white, yellow and other pigments were less enduring.

Where are the artists today? While the genetic inheritance is strong in the rural Western and Northern Cape, the San culture has virtually been obliterated. It's a tragic story of genocide, with many taken as servants, while others moved to the towns. Few retain their traditional culture but there's now an increasingly positive consciousness and, at last, pride among these descendants.

VITAL INFO

REGIONAL TOURISM BUREAUS

CERES TOURISM 023 316 1287, www.ceres.org.za

CLANWILLIAM TOURISM 027 482 2024, www.clanwilliam.info

LAMBERT'S BAY TOURISM 027 432 1000, www.lambertsbay.com

PAARL TOURISM 021 872 3829, www.paarlonline.com

WUPPERTHAL TOURISM 027 492 3410

ALL THE REST

BIRD ISLAND NATURE RESERVE Lambert's Bay, 022 931 2900. The island's accessible any time, but the bird hide and new visitors' complex is open daily 7:00–19:00 in summer and till 17:00 in winter.

BOSDUIFKLIP Lambert's Bay, 027 432 2735, lunch and dinner depending on bookings

CALABASH BUSH PUB, Bain's Kloof Pass, 023 355 1844, open daily 10:00 till the last person leaves at night

CEDERBERG PRIVATE CELLAR Cederberg, 027 482 2827, www.cederbergwine.com, open as for Dwarsrivier office, but closed Sun

MATJIESRIVIER NATURE RESERVE Cederberg, 027 482 2785, daily 7:30–13:00 and 13:30–16:00

MUISBOSSKERM Lambert's Bay, 027 432 1017, lunch and dinner daily, depending on reservations

PAARL MOUNTAIN NATURE RESERVE 021 872 3658, open Oct–March 7:00–19:00, April–Sept 7:00–18:00, entrance fee payable on weekends and public holidays

THE DUNES 4X4 ROUTE Lambert's Bay, 027 432 1244

WETHU EXPERIENCES in post office building, Op-die-Berg, 023 317 0625, www.wethu.com

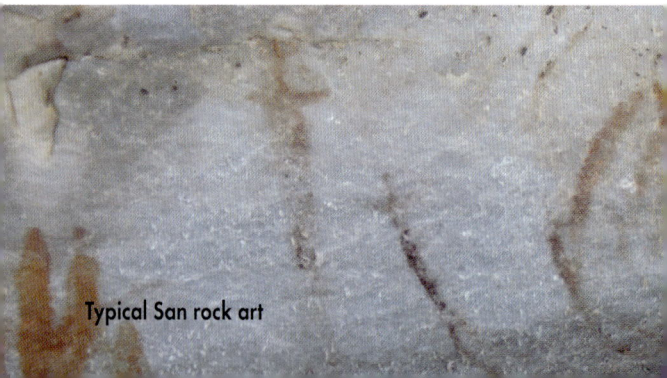

Typical San rock art

WHERE TO STAY:

ALGERIA Cederberg Wilderness Area, Western Cape Nature Conservation, 027 482 2403, office open Mon–Fri 7:30–16:00, gate open daily till 21:00, accommodation bookings 022 931 2088

BELMONT HOTEL Porter Street, Ceres, 023 312 1150, belmont@intekom.co.za, www.belmonthotel.co.za

BUSHMAN'S KLOOF WILDERNESS RESERVE off R364 near Clanwilliam, reservations 021 797 0990, lodge 027 482 2627, www.bushmanskloof.co.za

CEDERBERG OASIS BACKPACKERS 027 482 2819

DWARSRIVIER AND SANDDRIF Cederberg, 027 482 2825, office open Mon–Sat 8:00–12:30 and 14:00–17:00, Sun 9:00–12:00 and 16:00–18:00

KAGGA KAMMA PRIVATE GAME RESERVE about 50km north-east of Op-die-Berg, 021 872 4343, www.kaggakamma.co.za, entrance gates close at 18:30

KLEIN CEDERBERG GUESTHOUSE 023 317 0783

KROMRIVIER Cederberg, 027 482 2807/2822, www.cederberg.co.za

MOUNT CEDER between Cederberg and Op-die-Berg, 023 317 0848/0113, www.mountceder.co.za

NUWERUST 027 482 2813

RIETVLEI 023 317 0883

TRAVELLER'S REST HOLIDAY COTTAGES on R364 near Clanwilliam, 027 482 1824 (preferably phone 13:00–14:00 or after 20:00), travrest@clanwilliam.co.za

ZOO RIDGE 023 317 0852

Humpback whale breaching

THE ROUTE:

Watch aquabatic displays by southern rights who frolic along the coast from Gordon's Bay to Hermanus, Arniston and L'Agulhas, the southernmost tip of the African continent.

see MAP A

contact details on pp 192 & 193

TIME: This is a weekend route, but if you have the time, give yourself an extra night or two in Hermanus, especially if you want to do any boat trips or go diving with sharks, or opt for gentle indulgences like some wine tasting.

DISTANCE: Approx 420km, excluding driving within towns

BEST TIME TO GO: June to November is prime whale season, with calving in August and September, and whale numbers peaking in October. Spring in September and October turns the countryside into a spectacular kaleidoscope of floral colour.

whales

INTRODUCTION

Spectacular coastal scenery and mountain fynbos put on a fine show, but the stars of this route are the southern right whales that, between June and November each year, swap their chilly Antarctic feeding grounds for our warmer, protected bays where they mate, calve, breach and lobtail, sometimes just metres from the shore.

It's hard to imagine 60 tons of solid matter frolicking, but that's certainly what it looks like. Of course, experts have various theories, but we think they do it... well, because they can.

The route hugs the coast through the most crowded parts of this giant whale nursery, where in season you can see up to 20 at play at a time.

We weren't always this lucky – whale hunters took a devastating toll on numbers from the 1800s onwards, and as whales with calves were the main targets, the population plummeted. Thankfully the southern right became a protected species in 1935 and now the whales are back, with more and more returning to our shores each year. Enjoy the aquabatics in the bay, but even out of whale season, there's plenty in which to indulge and delight along this beautifully scenic route.

WHALE-WATCHING

✓ Unlike humpback and Bryde's whales, southern rights have no dorsal fin, and unless they're performing, they look more like hippos than whales. Recognise them by their callosities, those rough, whitish raised patches dotted around their heads.

✓ Hope for a calm, windless day, when whales tend to come closest to shore (although they're often more lazy then too). Blows are usually the first things you see. Whales are particularly obliging when breaching, as they tend to do it several times, allowing you to set up your camera!

whales

Cape Agulhas lighthouse

Spyhopping at the coast

THE ROUTE

Day One

- Scenic drive via Gordon's Bay and the Harold Porter National Botanical Garden to Hermanus
- Lunch while watching whale aquabatics in Walker Bay
- An afternoon of pleasure – whales, wines and shopping
- Overnight in Hermanus

Day Two

- Explore Stanford and visit a brewery
- Whale-watch through Die Kelders and Gansbaai
- Visit Elim, a national monument mission village
- Stand at the southern tip of Africa at L'Agulhas
- Overnight in Arniston, or fast-track back to Cape Town on the N2. Make this a longer adventure by linking this route to the Golf, Adrenalin or Country Routes via Swellendam

READING LIST

- ✓ *Hermanus Info* is a handy booklet available at tourism bureaus, with absolutely every detail and phone number.
- ✓ There are several good guides to whales, like *Whale Watch: A Guide to Whales and Other Marine Mammals of Southern Africa*, by Vic Cockcroft and Peter Joyce (Struik), and *Whale watching in South Africa*, by Peter Best (Mammal Research Institute, University of Pretoria).
- ✓ Peter Slingsby has produced a very helpful map called *The Overberg Whale Coast* (Baardskeerder), with information on Hermanus, Cape L'Agulhas and Swellendam.
- ✓ *Kogelberg Biosphere Reserve: Heart of the Cape Flora*, by Amida and Mark Johns (Struik).
- ✓ www.hermanus.co.za is packed with info.

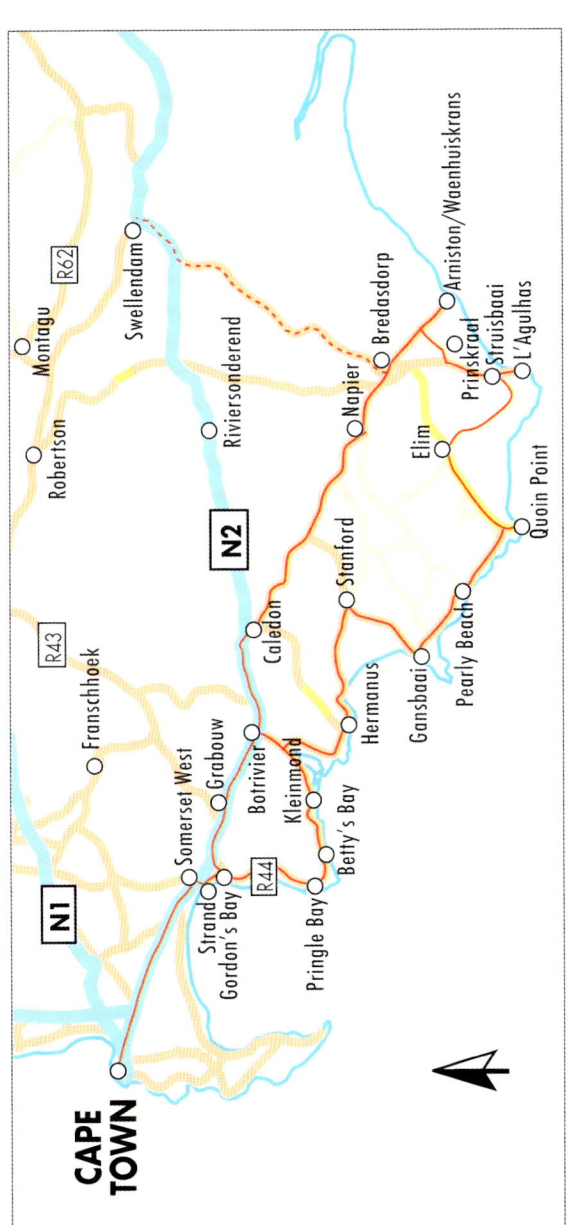

Blowing for the camera

ONE

Waterfront to Betty's Bay – 1hr 15min

From the Waterfront, turn left onto the highway following N1 Paarl then N2 Somerset West. At just over 40km, take Exit 43 Somerset West, Broadway Boulevard, Stellenbosch and turn right at the traffic lights onto R44. (Alternatively, skip Strand and stay on the N2 till about 50km, turning right to Kleinmond and Gordon's Bay, but the following mileages are based on the route via Strand.) At the third set of lights turn right into Beach Road to Strand Beachfront. Turn right at circle, right again at the traffic light (50km) onto R44, Gordon's Bay road. When road splits at about 53km fork right to Faure Street, signed Bikini Beach. Follow Gordon's Bay Beachfront, T-junction right (R44), and watch False Bay unfold before you.

A warm water whale route could start in Muizenberg, following the coast road all along the curve of False Bay, but for those lacking the time, remember there's really good stuff ahead, so

WHALE SPOTTING IN CAPE TOWN

- ✓ Boyes Drive above Muizenberg and Kalk Bay
- ✓ Main road between Glencairn and Simon's Town
- ✓ From Boulders to Cape Point, especially Miller's and Partridge points
- ✓ Above Noordhoek, in Chapman's Bay
- ✓ In Hout Bay, from the Chapman's Peak Drive viewsites
- ✓ Along the drive between Llandudno and Sea Point

brave the freeway frenzy to fast-track to the Strand (Afrikaans for 'Beach'), Gordon's Bay and the scenic Clarence Drive.

From Gordon's Bay, the Hottentots Holland mountains almost trip over this serpentine road as they tumble into the sea. Across False Bay you can see the spiny ridge of the Table Mountain chain snaking all the way to Cape Point in the far distance, and here's where you can start whale-watching in earnest – in season there's a good chance of seeing a whale or two lazing in the sea below. Clarence Drive flashes past the holiday village of Rooiels (named after the red alders that used to grow here), to

179

the turn-off to Pringle Bay and Cape Hangklip, where the road leaves the sea for a while to make a detour inland.

The steep sentinel of Cape Hangklip (Overhanging Rock) marks the abrupt end of the Hottentots Holland mountain range, whose caves and valleys were once a refuge for slaves who escaped their owners in Cape Town.

Betty's Bay straggles along for several kilometres, in the middle of which you'll come upon the Harold Porter National Botanical Garden, a great, fynbos-filled place to take a break (entrance fee charged). There's a tearoom, a souvenir shop, a great indigenous nursery and a plant information centre. The beautiful gardens have several walks which meander among the waterfalls and pools that form a chain down to the sea.

DID YOU KNOW?

Not many Capetonians do: The mountains above Gordon's Bay (named after Captain Robert Gordon who explored the area in 1778) bear an anchor and a large GB picked out in big, whitewashed stones. But the GB is not actually for Gordon's Bay, according to author TV Bulpin, it stands for the General Botha Training College, as the naval academy was originally called.

Lobtailing

Betty's Bay to Hermanus – 40min

Continue along the R44, passing Kleinmond at about 99km. At the T-junction turn right on the R43 to Hermanus. Pass Fisherhaven, Hawston, Vermont, Onrus River. Enter Hermanus at about 132km. At 135km, you're forced left at the traffic lights. Turn next right into Market Street, right again into Kusweg and park on Market Square.

Hermanus is the self-styled centre of the whale-watching universe, tucked into the most protected corner of Walker Bay, which has been recognised by the World Wide Fund for Nature (WWF) as one of the world's top 12 whale-viewing sites. The town has a fun – if busy – buzz, especially in season, and you'll almost always find the rocks thronged with people staring out to sea, not daring to blink in case they miss a breach. You can also get up close and personal. These marine giants sometimes come within 10 metres of the shore, so haul out your binoculars and get a front row seat.

If you're hungry by now you can whale-watch over your plate of seafood at several sea-view restaurants on Market Square overlooking the Old Harbour.

Sit outdoors at The Burgundy or walk a couple of hundred metres further, with the sea on your right, and then down some

stairs to Bientang's Cave, a restaurant built in a cave, once home to a Strandloper, immediately above the rocks and waves. You can't get closer to the whales than this.

But if you can't see any whales, just listen. Hermanus is the only town in the world that employs a whale crier, Wilson Salukazana, who blows a kind of Morse code on a kelp horn to indicate exactly where the whales are. You'll spot him walking along the coastal cliff, wearing sandwich boards that explain the code.

Spend the afternoon watching whale aquabatics, wandering around town or doing some of this good stuff:

- Hit the water and go whale-watching by boat. Licensed operators are allowed within 50 metres of a whale (private boats must stay 300 metres away), but there's every chance the whales will come closer to take a look at you. There are two operators based at the New Harbour. Follow the coast road (Kusweg) with the sea on your left for about three kilometres to the New Harbour. Try Southern Right Charters on Miroshga, a slick speed boat (with a toilet) which zips along the coast to where the whales are, or there's Hermanus Whale Cruises, in an authentic fishing boat. More info on other operators available from the tourism bureau.

- To get the big picture, take a quick spin up the spectacular Rotary Way, which winds up into the mountains above

the town, from where you can watch paragliders and hang-gliders leap into the air, and get awesome 180-degree views across the bay. From Market Square, turn right into Harbour Road and head out of Hermanus. Turn right after about two and a half kilometres, between white gateposts. Road becomes good gravel on the plateau at around six kilometres; either turn back, or loop back to town through the Hamilton Russell Vineyards, turning left after you go through their gates, and dropping down into the Hemel-en-Aarde Valley. Stop for a tasting! The entire loop, ending back on Market Square in town, is 22 kilometres long.

- Do the Hermanus Wine Wander where five estates make unique wines due to the cool climate and proximity to the sea. All have beautiful views of the Hemel-en-Aarde ('Heaven and Earth') Valley, offer tastings, and most do cellar tours by appointment, so give them a call before you arrive. WhaleHaven is first, then Hamilton Russell Vineyards are about five kilometres later, followed almost immediately by Bouchard Finlayson. Next up is Cape Bay, infinitely easier on South African pockets, followed by the newest, Sumaridge Wines, which also has a restaurant. Go via Rotary Way or continue past that turn-off until you can turn right to R320

DID YOU KNOW?

Southern rights were so named as they were the 'right' whales to catch. They yielded the most oil and, when killed, were obliging enough to float, making them easy to get to shore.

GOOD TO KNOW

Hermanus Pieters was a shepherd and teacher who one day in the 1830s followed the Olifants Pad (Elephant's Way) out of the Hemel-en-Aarde Valley and looked down on an unspoilt stretch of coast. He camped at a spring (or 'fontein', in Afrikaans) close to the waves, and loved it so much he began to return each summer. People still do the same, even though Hermanuspietersfontein has now been shortened to Hermanus.

Caledon (four kilometres). The R320 becomes gravel after 10 kilometres, and reaches Caledon on the N2 at 38 kilometres.

- Do the coastal Cliff Path walk, whale-watching all the way from the New Harbour past town to Grotto Beach. It's about 12 kilometres in all, with a wheelchair-friendly section in the middle, between the Windsor and Marine hotels.

- Market Square bustles with gift shops, galleries and restaurants, with a lively craft market over weekends. The roads and alleys leading off the square are packed with interesting bookstores, galleries and antique shops.

- Fernkloof Nature Reserve packs over 1 100 species of

Seal colony at Geyser Rock near Dyer Island

coastal mountain fynbos into its 15 square kilometres (the entire United Kingdom has 1 500 species!), including rare and unusual plants of international scientific interest. There are over 50 kilometres of graded paths and trails, amid beautiful fynbos and ericas, an indigenous plant nursery and a mountain bike trail. From Market Square follow Kusweg with the sea on your right, and turn right into Main Road. Turn left to Fernkloof at about three kilometres.

- Grab a game of 18 holes at Arabella Golf Estate, see the Golf Route, pp 225–226.
- Take an Ubuntu Cultural Tour through Zwelihle township with the whale crier, Wilson Salukazana, for a taste of African hospitality, shopping at a spaza and downing a quick ale in a local shebeen. Visits with dancers, singers and traditional healers can also be arranged.
- Grotto Beach, Voëlklip and Kammabaai, all in the direction of Stanford, are great beaches for soaking up the sun.
- De Wet's Huis Photo Museum on the square, is filled with old images of Hermanus, while the Old Harbour Museum,

depicting the history of fishing and whaling in the area, is across the road at the water's edge.

- Don't forget to ask the tourism bureau about fishing as well as fly-fishing, scuba diving, boating, kayaking, 4x4 routes, paragliding and hiking the stunning five-day Whale Trail through De Hoop Nature Reserve.

TWO

Hermanus to Stanford – 30min

From the monument on the square, take the Main Road (which becomes the R43) out of Hermanus, following signs for Stanford, Gansbaai. At about 23km, turn right into Stanford.

It takes a while to leave Hermanus as the town sprawls for several kilometres along Walker Bay, then there's a really pretty stretch of road with the mountains on your left and Kleinriviervlei on the right before you turn to Stanford. This is a delightful,

L'AGULHAS

Initially called Cape St Brendan by the famous Portuguese explorer Bartholomeu Dias in 1488, L'Agulhas came to be so named as compass needles (or 'agulhas' in Portuguese) show no magnetic deviation from true north here.

sleepy country village that seems poised to become the next tourist hotspot. A walk around might tempt you back here for a weekend because there's certainly plenty to do:

- The Birkenhead Brewery is an exclusive micro-brewery, restaurant and pub with beautiful views. Tour the brewery and taste their beers – a lager, a kolsch, a traditional German wheat beer and a 'chocolate' milk stout. Ask the brewmaster to explain how beer is actually slimming...

- Enjoy the birdlife on a stroll along the Klein River, hire a boat from Klein River Boat Hire, or take a cruise. The African Queen River Cruises accommodates up to 40 people, while the smaller Platanna River Trips take eight to nine.

- People drive all the way from Cape Town to eat at Mariana's Deli and Bistro at Owl's Barn. She offers home-grown organic ingredients (where possible) and you can choose from a wide selection of freshly baked breads, pastas, mustards and salad dressings to take home with you.

Stanford to Elim – 1hr 20min

At four-way stop, continue along R43 through Gansbaai. Ignore first turn to Elim, Baardskeerdersbos. At 54km, take left on gravel to Elim, Bredasdorp, Struisbaai, and L'Agulhas. Fork left to Elim at 60km. At T-junction (64km), take left to Elim, Wolvengat. Follow curve of the road to the right. Enter Elim at 77km; park at the church.

The road turns back towards the sea after Stanford, and there are excellent whale-watching opportunities all along Die Kelders to Gansbaai and Danger Point, the rocky promontory infamous for wrecking HMS *Birkenhead* in February 1852, with the loss of 445 lives. On board were British soldiers whose stoic bravery in standing on deck as the ship foundered, while civilians climbed aboard the few lifeboats, has gone down in maritime history as the Birkenhead Drill – women and children first. The turn-off to Danger Point, about one kilometre beyond Gansbaai, takes you to a lighthouse and a blowhole that, in really rough seas, can shoot a plume of water up to 10 metres high. Birkenhead Rock can be seen at low tide.

The need for bravery has remained in Gansbaai, especially if you're up for climbing into a metal cage to dive with the sharks! Gansbaai is regarded as one of the best shark-diving sites in the world, so do give it a go.

Elim is a quaint Moravian Mission station. The church owns the entire village and only members may live there. Established in 1824, Elim is a national monument and it's really as if time has stood still. But the church clock hasn't. It's the oldest working clock in South Africa (built in Germany in 1764) and it's unusual in that it has faces on both ends of the church – a solid axle runs the length of the building, connecting the two gables.

Opposite the church is South Africa's only monument celebrating the emancipation of slaves. It's seriously low-key, but definitely unique. Although slavery was abolished in the Cape in 1834, the monument is dated 1838 as slaves were forced to work a further four years to 'buy' their freedom.

Quite a few Elim locals can trace their ancestry back to the original German missionaries, some of whom even sold themselves into slavery to spread the word! Ask the tourism bureau about guided tours, accommodation and lunch bookings.

Elim to L'Agulhas – 50min

Just past the church, take right to Bredasdorp, Struisbaai, L'Agulhas. At 34km, T-junction right to R319 Struisbaai, L'Agulhas on tar. Keep straight through Struisbaai to L'Agulhas lighthouse at 46km.

The gravel road leaving Elim goes through beautiful farmlands stretching to the dusty purple Bredasdorp mountains in the distance. Slow down to look at some original whitewashed fishermen's houses on either side as you enter Struisbaai. They're all national monuments and are generally two-roomed, with thick lime-washed walls and a thatched roof, often with a fat chimney and oven at one end. These cottages are known as Hotagterklip ('Left Behind the Stone'), after a rocky outcrop that caused a sharp detour on the original wagon route. Struisbaai also boasts a stunning beach that sweeps around the bay.

What L'Agulhas may lack in architectural charm, it makes up for in geographic fame – this is the southernmost point of the African continent, and the waves pounding these rugged rocks mark the confluence of the Indian and Atlantic oceans – just don't tell that to all the Cape Town-based operations with 'Two Oceans' in their names. The precise point is marked by a plaque about one kilometre past the lighthouse. Walk the last 150 metres to the nondescript rock that's one of the most photographed in the world. It's worth climbing the lighthouse tower not only for the view, but to glimpse the surprisingly tiny light bulb that nevertheless pumps out the light equivalent of seven and a half million candles. Make time for the museum, which sheds light on the history of lighthouses around the country, not only this one. After your climb up the tower, rest up in the restaurant. There are also a couple of pubs and restaurants in L'Agulhas itself.

L'Agulhas to Arniston/Waenhuiskrans – 55min

Return through L'Agulhas and Struisbaai. At 23km, turn right on gravel to Arniston/Waenhuiskrans, De Mond, Prinskraal. At Prinskraal (30km), T-junction left then immediately right to Arniston. At 37km, T-junction to the right on tar R316 Arniston. At 43km, turn left at stop street to Arniston Hotel.

The gravel road does a left-right dogleg through a farmyard at Prinskraal. Look out for ostriches in a paddock a little further on.

Arniston, if you can see past the sprawling developments that are mushrooming here, is an enchanting fishing village of great beauty, with authentic fishermen's cottages on the hill, deep blue sea and a long beach for tranquil walks. And take your binoculars because this part of the coast also has the biggest concentration of whale cow-and-calf pairs in the country.

Arniston's official name is Waenhuiskrans ('Wagon House Cliff'), after a huge sea cave that local settlers said was big enough to shelter several wagons and their oxen. It's an easy 20-minute walk to the cave (about two kilometres) – best is along the seafront with its rocky shelves, arches and eroded rocks, or you can go by road. It's only accessible at low tide for a couple of hours so check with a local resident for the best time to go.

The town's English name comes from the HMS *Arniston*, which was en route from Ceylon to England, loaded with wounded soldiers and 39 women and children, when it was wrecked in this bay in 1815. Only six of the 378 people on board made it to shore, where they waited two weeks before they were found.

Brave enough?

There are several shark diving and boat-based whale-watching operators based in Gansbaai; four in particular are recommended:

- ✓ Marine Dynamics lets you come face to face with Jaws while dangling safely in a cage. *National Geographic*, *50/50*, *Time* magazine and the Discovery Channel have used them, so you probably can too.

- ✓ White Shark Adventures aims to raise awareness and change people's attitude to great whites. Ask operator Jackie Smit about his fight to the death with a shark.

- ✓ Dyer Island Cruises focuses on whales, but they're always ready to take a look at great white sharks and you may well see these mighty sharks leaping right out of the water to catch a seal for supper.

- ✓ Ivanhoe Sea Safaris is a bit of a legend among the whale-watchers, who say the whales have learnt to recognise the sound of this engine and come up to greet the boat. Who knows? Why not see for yourself?

whales

There's a monument in memory of some of the passengers a few hundred metres from the hotel.

More to do
around Arniston:
- The lovely craft centre at Kassiesbaai (within easy walking distance)
- Angling, squash, cycling, birdwatching, aircraft hire and microlighting
- The Shipwreck Museum in Bredasdorp commemorates the hundreds of ships that have been wrecked along this treacherous coastline
- De Hoop Nature Reserve, for coastal and fynbos walks, and whale sightings from Koppie Alleen between May and November
- Golf as well as tennis at Bredasdorp
- Hot springs and the casino at Caledon

Arniston to Cape Town – 2hr 20min
Follow R316 through Bredasdorp (follow signs to R316 Caledon), through Napier into Caledon at 94km. Turn left onto N2 Kaapstad (Cape Town) at 96km. Follow N2 over Sir Lowry's Pass to the city. Or turn right on N2 to link up with the Golf Route or the Adrenalin Route: At Bredasdorp, follow the signs to N2 Swellendam.

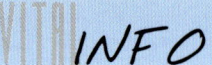

PHONE THE HERMANUS WHALE CRIER Wilson Salukazana,
for an on-the-spot update on where the whales are,
073 214 6949 (June to November)

24-HOUR WHALE ROUTE INFORMATION LINE 083 910 1028

BETTY'S BAY

HAROLD PORTER NATIONAL BOTANICAL GARDEN R44, Betty's Bay,
028 272 9311, http://www.nbi.ac.za, open daily 8:00–18:00

HERMANUS

BIENTANG'S CAVE below Marine Drive, 028 312 3454, daily 11:30–16:00,
if enough bookings, Fri & Sat nights 18:30–late

BOUCHARD FINLAYSON VINEYARDS AND CELLARS 028 312 3515,
www.bouchardfinlayson.co.za, weekdays 9:00–17:00, Sat 9:30–12:30

CAPE BAY WINES 028 312 3862, weekdays 9:00–16:00, Sat 10:00–12:30

FERNKLOOF NATURE RESERVE 028 313 8100, www.fernkloof.com

HAMILTON RUSSELL VINEYARDS 028 312 3595, weekdays 9:00–13:00 and
14:00–17:00, Sat 9:00–13:00

HERMANUS WHALE CRUISES 028 315 1406

SOUTHERN RIGHT CHARTERS 082 353 0550

SUMARIDGE WINES 028 312 1097, www.sumaridge.co.za, Mon–Sat
10:00–15:00, Sun in season

**THE WESTERN CAPE HOTEL AND SPA – ARABELLA GOLF ESTATE AND
ALTIRA SPA** 028 284 0000, www.arabellasheraton.com/westerncape

THE BURGUNDY on Market Square 028 312 2800, open daily 8:30–16:15,
19:00–late, closed on Sun nights

UBUNTU CULTURAL TOURS OF ZWELIHLE TOWNSHIP 073 214 6949,
028 312 4334/2629

WHALEHAVEN WINES 028 316 1633, www.whalehavenwines.co.za,
weekdays 9:30–17:00, Sat 10:30–14:00

STANFORD

AFRICAN QUEEN RIVER CRUISES 082 732 1284

BIRKENHEAD BREWERY 028 341 0183, www.birkenhead.co.za, open daily
11:00–17:00, Fri, Sat and Sun 18:00–22:00 in season

KLEIN RIVER BOAT HIRE 028 341 0404, 083 248 5827

KLEIN RIVER CHEESE 028 341 0693, open Mon–Fri 9:00–17:00, Sat
9:00–13:00

MARIANA'S DELI AND BISTRO 028 341 0272, open Fri, Sat, Sun 9:00–16:00
PLATANNA RIVER TRIPS 082 353 0588

GANSBAAI
DYER ISLAND CRUISES (whale cruises) 082 801 8014
GREAT WHITE HOUSE (shark and whale cruises) 028 384 3273
IVANHOE SEA SAFARIS (whale-watching) 028 384 0556
MARINE DYNAMICS (shark diving) 028 384 1005
WHITE SHARK ADVENTURES (shark diving) 028 384 1380

ELIM
ELIM MILL TEAROOM AND ELIM GUESTHOUSE 028 482 1806

L'AGULHAS
CAPE AGULHAS LIGHTHOUSE AND MUSEUM 028 435 6600, open daily 9:00–16:45

REGIONAL TOURISM BUREAUS
OVERBERG TOURISM Caledon, 028 214 1466
HERMANUS TOURISM Mitchell Street, 028 312 2629
STANFORD TOURISM 17 Queen Victoria Street, 028 341 0340
GANSBAAI TOURISM cnr Berg & Main roads, 028 384 1439
ELIM TOURISM BUREAU 028 482 1806
SUIDPUNT TOURISM (L'AGULHAS, STRUISBAAI, ARNISTON) Dr Jansen Street, Bredasdorp, 028 424 2584

WHERE TO STAY:

HERMANUS
AUBERGE BURGUNDY 028 313 1201, www.auberge.co.za
BIRKENHEAD HOUSE 028 314 8000, www.birkenheadhouse.com

ARNISTON
ARNISTON HOTEL 028 445 9000, www.arnistonhotel.com
ARNISTON SEASIDE COTTAGES 028 445 9772, www.arniston-online.co.za

Bungee jumping off Bloukrans Bridge

THE ROUTE:
Take a deep breath – we're going to fly off Signal Hill, dangle off Table Mountain, swim with multi-fanged predators and jump the world's highest bungee along the Garden Route. Are you up for it?

see MAPS A & B

contact details on pp 214 & 215

TIME: Three nights, four days

DISTANCE: Approx 800km one way (add about 500km for direct return to Cape Town)

BEST TIME TO GO: Definitely all year, though these activities are generally outdoors and weather-permitting, so the summery fine weather from November to April is best.

adrenalin

INTRODUCTION

Say goodbye to your comfort zone, you're about to OD on undiluted adrenalin. We hope you have a head for heights because there's abseiling at either end of this route – the first off Table Mountain, the last off the Knysna Heads – with plenty of white-knuckled paragliding, shark-diving and bungee jumping action in between. In fact, whatever your preferred adrenalin rush, here's your fix, so brace yourself and, whatever you do, never, ever, look before you leap.

READING LIST

- ✓ The *Getaway Adventure Guide*, by Jennifer Stern (Ramsay, Son and Parker), lists adventure activities not only in South Africa, but also Botswana, Namibia, Zambia, Malawi, Mozambique, Zimbabwe, Lesotho and Swaziland.

- ✓ If you want something really scary, get *Extreme Ironing* by Phil Shaw (New Holland), but it's only for people who take their housekeeping seriously.

Bungee star jump

Mountain biking

THE ROUTE

Day One
- Abseil off Table Mountain, or
- Tandem paraglide wherever the wind blows, or
- Try a high speed mountain bike ride on the slopes of Table Mountain, or
- Free-climb a 32-graded route at City Rock (okay, you can top-rope it)
- Overnight in Cape Town

Day Two
- Bridge (or bungee) jump off the Gouritz River Bridge
- Dive with great white sharks at Mossel Bay
- Overnight in Mossel Bay

Day Three
- Try a deep dive off Plettenberg Bay, or a spring tide dive between the Knysna Heads
- Tackle the world's highest bungee off Bloukrans Bridge
- Cable slide from tree to tree in indigenous forest
- Sail through Knysna Heads
- Overnight in Knysna

Day Four
- An awesome foursome in Knysna – kayak across the lagoon, ride quadbikes, abseil over the sea then rap jump off the Heads
- Chill out on a slow drive back to Cape Town on the N2 or take an extra day or two and return to Cape Town on Route 62 via Oudtshoorn

BEFORE YOU GO

- ✓ The scuba dives require a minimum Openwater One qualification. Bring your card as operators will not let you dive without it.
- ✓ It's vital to book first and remember that all outdoor options are weather permitting.
- ✓ Shark Africa, the Mossel Bay cage dive operation, closes from early December to mid-January.
- ✓ The tandem paraglide is dependent on current conditions and wind direction. So book that first and schedule other activities around it.

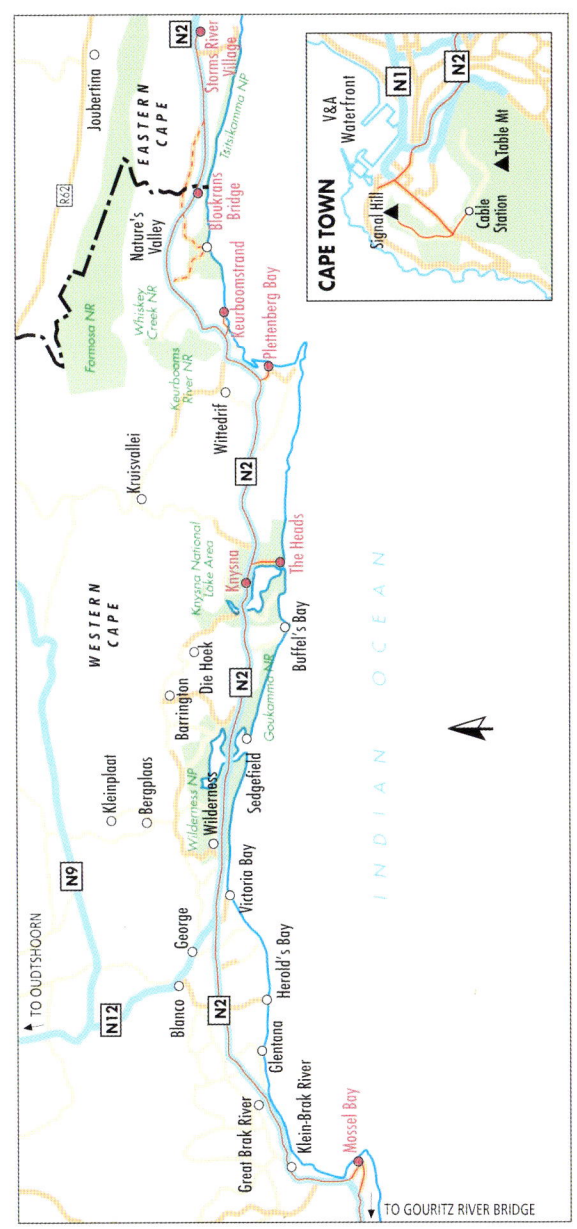

ONE

Waterfront to Table Mountain – 12min

From the Waterfront turn right into Buitengracht (M62 Camps Bay) and follow cableway signs. At about 4.5km turn left into Tafelberg Road. The lower cable station is about 1.5km further.

What is it about mountains that makes people (well, the slightly insane) want to leap off them? Here's the ultimate in 'yes, I really did this' – step right off the edge of Table Mountain, a world heritage site and Cape Town's most loved icon. Abseil Africa operates the Western Cape's highest natural abseil from a rocky and seriously exposed perch close to the upper cable station. It's an awesome 112 metres long and if that sounds like kid's stuff, bear in mind that there's a whole lot of nothing between you and the sea, 1 063 metres below. After donning a harness, listening to a quick safety briefing (which includes

Bakoven from Kasteelspoort, Table Mountain

useful advice such as 'remain calm at all times') and having a quick practice on a static line, you're set to go. The take-off point has a spectacular view over Camps Bay and Clifton. Enjoy it, as it's probably the last thing you see before you step off the edge, your brain shuts down and fear takes over.

Then, just as you begin to realise how exposed you feel, bouncing off a sheer cliff 1 000 metres up, it gets a whole lot worse. The cliff vanishes into an overhang, and you're left dangling (with another 60-odd metres to go) in mid-air. This is guaranteed to get your attention. It could be worse, though. You're now abseiling more or less down the line of South Africa's toughest rock climb, graded 33, which has been climbed by only a handful of very brave people, who have thoughtfully called it 'Mary Poppins' Giant Umbrella', due to the length of time spent hanging from one knuckle as they try to negotiate their way up the overhang.

WHEN THE WEATHER WON'T LET YOU PLAY

Head indoors and push your limits at City Rock, South Africa's largest indoor climbing gym. There are 450m of wall (and ceiling) dotted with handholds (some jugs, some barely there), to keep you going till the weather clears. All the routes are graded from an easy 8 to a barely possible 32, which spiders its way along the roof. It's guaranteed to get you pumped!

There's gear for hire or take your own, and staff will belay you (and help with technique) for an extra fee. Two–hour beginners' courses are available if all this is new to you. See Kids' Route, pp 120–121.

The average time for the abseil is about 10 minutes, then there's an easy, half-hour walk that gently climbs back up to the top. No experience is necessary. The abseil is, of course, weather-dependent. One of the best things about this abseil is that they have two ropes side-by-side, so if you think you'll be lonely out there, do it with a friend.

If you prefer going up rather than plummeting down, try mountain climbing with Out There Facilitation. They'll find a route to suit your experience and need for adrenalin, covering the basics for novices who're still learning the ropes, to guided sport and traditional ascents for accomplished climbers. They also guide kloofing and hiking routes.

Taking a breather

Want to go higher? Okay, get ready for take-off...

Imagine the serenity of soaring higher than eagles while surrounded by spectacular beauty, the silence broken only by the rush of the air. And all this from the comfort of a Lazee-Boy of sorts. Armchair travelling has never been this good.

The quick-fix for wanna-be paragliders is to do it in tandem, strapped to a pilot who'll do all the flying while you settle back in the harness and put your feet up. And the in-flight entertainment will take your breath away, as you float on thermals, a weightless wisp of freedom in a blue world of sea and sky. Good news if you have a height phobia: some say the serenity gets to you, and although you're high up, the feeling of vertigo disappears as you're not on the edge of anything. Go on, give it a go.

Local operators have formed a joint company called the Air Team, which co-ordinates all the paragliding options. Depending on the wind direction, you may take off from Signal Hill, Lion's Head, Sir Lowry's Pass, Franschhoek or Hermanus (allow a full day for the last two destinations), or Porterville (overnight trip). No experience is necessary – you'll get a full briefing and all the required gear, and flights usually last between 15 minutes and half an hour. A word of caution: there are various paragliders willing to take you for a ride. Before leaving the safety of planet earth, make sure your pilot has a tandem-rated paragliding licence and insurance that covers you as a passenger.

Waterfront to Kloof Street – 8min

From the Waterfront turn right into Buitengracht (M62 Camps Bay) and follow cableway signs. After 2km turn left into Buitensingel Road, then straight through traffic lights. Downhill Adventures is on the right.

If you're more of a speed demon than a height head, here's your fix: scream down Table Mountain on a hi-tech mountain bike, flashing past the fynbos with nothing between you and the world but wind and a sturdy helmet.

Allow half a day (at least three hours) for the guided Table Mountain Double Descent from Downhill Adventures. The route starts at the lower cable station on Tafelberg Road, then hurtles off-road along a jeep track, traversing the slopes on a downhill rollercoaster, with fabulous views of the City Bowl, Lion's Head, Devil's Peak and Table Bay.

Of course, a double-descent means at some point you need to go up again, but with 21 gears the cycle back up to Tafelberg Road is quick. Saving the best for last, the route veers off-road again from the end of the tar, with a long downhill race into Vredehoek. You need to behave once again on the tar road down into the city before ending at the shop.

Downhill Adventures will supply bikes, helmets and water, but you need to bring closed shoes. The route suits advanced riders (who'll go faster) as well as absolute beginners – no experience required although you must be able to ride a bike.

Another mountain biking option is Daytrippers who, aside from routes below Table Mountain, have various tours around the Peninsula and the Cape Winelands, where you cycle between wine estates.

TWO

Waterfront to
Gouritz Bridge – approx 3hr 50min

From the Waterfront turn left onto the highway, following N1 Paarl then N2 Somerset West. Remain on N2 (Caledon, Mossel Bay, George) for 340km. Gouritz Bridge is about 16km after Albertinia.

This is where bungee jumping began in South Africa but with

bigger plunges later on, get into the swing of things with the bridge swing. As you teeter on the edge of the jump platform, look across to the new road bridge – that's where your lifeline is attached. This is much better than looking down into the river bed way, way below. Then, leaving your stomach behind, dive/leap/fall off, and feel the rush as you freefall and pendulum through the air. If you want to get closer to your partner than ever before, do the bridge swing in tandem.

Wear walking shoes for once you've swung to a stop, you're lowered to the ground to walk up out of the gorge. There's an age limit of 14 years and a minimum weight of 40kg. Under-18s must get parental consent.

Now that you're back on terra firma, be prepared to leave it behind again. We're off to play with some predators.

Gouritz to Mossel Bay – 20min

Continue into Mossel Bay. Follow road left down the hill and turn right into Marsh Street, then left into Church Street. Mossel Bay Tourism is on the corner of Church and Market streets. Or follow the sharks signs from Marsh Street.

The alarming thing about the steel cage that's dangled off the edge of Shark Africa's catamaran is the rather large viewing port, which might look to a shark like a handy feeding hatch.

Comfort yourself that it's standard size and there have been no incidents. So

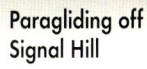

Paragliding off Signal Hill

far. Just don't lean out. Shark Africa sails out to Seal Island (home to about 4 000 seals) where they anchor, set bait and wait. It could be anything from five minutes to three hours before the great whites come; then, geared with a wetsuit, mask and air supply, you're lowered into the cage to go face to face with Jaws (who may be anything from twice your height to a mind-blowing six metres long). You don't need any dive qualifications and there are no age limits (youngest so far was five years, and oldest eighty-eight). Rates include gear, and you pay less if you're planning to watch from the boat. If you don't see any sharks, you get half your money back! Bank on spending up to five hours at sea.

More to do in Mossel Bay: Parasailing; microlighting; 4x4ing on the Vleesbaai Dune Route; game viewing; scenic flights; fly-fishing; whale-watching cruises to Seal Island; quadbiking (also game drives on quads); and helicopter trips.

THREE

Mossel Bay to Knysna – 1hr 15min

Watch your speed – there are lots of speed traps along here. Leave Mossel Bay following signs to N2 George, Hartenbos. Go through

FEAR FACTOR

Gansbaai, near Hermanus, is another worldfamous shark diving spot. See the Whale Route, p 190.

Wilderness and Sedgefield. Knysna Tourism is on the left at 106km. At 108km turn right into George Rex Drive and follow the signs to the Knysna Heads.

The treacherous sea between the Knysna Heads ups the fear factor on the drift dive offered by The Heads Diving Adventure Centre. It's a shore-entry at the Heads, then you drift down the channel with the current and over the wreck of the *Paquita*, an iron barge that was claimed by the Heads a hundred years ago. But perhaps drift is misleading: at spring high tide (the best time for this dive), you scream in at 12 knots. So there's no stopping – anything you grab hold of is coming with you. You can more or less choose your depth, from five to eight metres in the current, or dropping down into the channel at 16 to 18 metres, with the wreck at around eight metres. The Knysna lagoon is home to the extremely rare *Hippocampus capensis*, more recognisably known as the mystical sea horse, where you'll find them especially beneath Thesen's Jetty.

Openwater One dive qualification with experience is required; advanced is recommended.

If diving isn't your kind of thing, The Heads Diving Adventure Centre also offers township tours and canoe safaris up the

Knysna River into the forest. Abseiling, rap jumping, sea kayaking and paintball are also on the menu.

More to do in Knysna: Leisure Island, or Knysna Heads beaches (when snorkelling, don't go out in the channel); abseiling next to a waterfall in Kaaimans Gorge; houseboats on the lagoon; the Knysna Elephant Park; and the famed Outeniqua Choo-Tjoe, a unique steam train that puffs and blows between George and Knysna every day.

The week-long Knysna Oyster Festival, held in July, includes a marathon and various cycle races.

Mossel Bay to Plettenberg Bay – 1hr 40min

Follow route to Knysna (above) and keep straight through the town. At 138km turn right into Plettenberg Bay and keep straight to the sea. You'll see the Beacon Isle Hotel at the bottom of the hill; cross the river to get there.

Deep-dive junkies will love Whale Rock, at the tip of the Robberg Peninsula off Plettenberg Bay. It's one massive rock whose pinnacle just clears the water and then drops down a full 35 metres. Here's where the deep blue sea meets land for the first time, so, as operator Robin says, things are big out here.

Robberg Peninsula supports a seal colony, so you'll definitely see them on the surface and there's a good chance of diving with them swimming all around you. And of course seals attract great white sharks, which have also been seen on dives. (Advanced dive qualification required.) Whale Rock is one of several Plettenberg Bay dives offered from the Beacon Isle Hotel, operated by The Heads Adventure Diving Centre.

Scuba diving

More to do in Plettenberg Bay: Skydiving; glider trip; eco-marine cruises to see whales and dolphins; Monkey Land Primate Sanctuary; fishing; horse riding; canoe trips up the Keurbooms River; golf; polo; and a visit to a traditional mampoer and witblits distillery.

Knysna/Plettenberg Bay to Bloukrans – 50min/25min

Continue on the N2 towards Port Elizabeth. Cross Bloukrans Bridge about 70km from Knysna, or 30km from Plett. Turn left to Face Adrenalin after 500m.

Once you've dried off from your dive, face your fears on the world's highest commercial bungee jump off the 216-metre Bloukrans Bridge. You won't even notice the jaw-dropping beauty of the Tsitsikamma forest and gorge below as you inch your way to the middle of the bridge (you get there via a catwalk suspended beneath the road surface – and by coincidence it's also 216 metres to the middle). Five, four, three, two, one BUNGEE! And you've got five heart-stopping seconds to wonder whether you're actually attached to anything. An instructor will help winch you back up to the platform for the walk back.

Minimum weight for jumping is 45 kilograms, with a bottom age limit of 14 years, and some medical conditions may rule out a jump. Under-18s must get parental consent.

The Bloukrans bungee is really a three-in-one bargain. The first stomach-lurching drop is up to 180 metres. After the rebound, your second drop at 111 metres is higher than the Victoria Falls bungee. And at 65 metres, your third is longer than Gouritz.

The operators are Face Adrenalin, who also offer a stunning 200-metre flying fox slide (between the concrete pillars beneath the bridge). If you aren't brave enough to bungee, can you walk the walk? Try the bridge walk, à la Sydney Harbour bridge, where you do the catwalk to the bungee-viewing platforms – it's enclosed with netting but not solid, so you can see the gorge way down beneath your feet.

Bloukrans to Storms River Village – 10min

As you continue on the N2, ignore turn to Storms River Mouth. At about 13km turn right to Storms River Village. At T-junction, turn left to Storms River Adventures.

If you feel you can't take any more fear, the fun kicks in for the Tree-top Canopy Tour with Storms River Adventures (who also do river cruises, abseiling, river tubing, mountain biking, fishing, scuba diving and guided hikes).

The two- to three-hour (depending on numbers) canopy tour, one of only three in the entire world, is a huge flying fox slide that sets you swinging from tree to towering tree in the indigenous Tsitsikamma forest, a good 30 to 45 metres above ground. Secure in a harness and hitched to a sturdy steel cable, you launch yourself from the tops of giant yellowwoods, seeing (if you're lucky) the shy Knysna louries at bird's-eye level. It's a whole new world up there, and once you've tasted it, you're not going to want to come down.

Storms River Village
to Keurboomstrand – 30min

From Storms River Adventures, return to N2 and turn left to George. After 10km, turn right onto the R102 Coldstream, George (or stay straight on N2 direct to Knysna). Bloukrans Pass is at 21km. Remain on R102 across bridge for Grootrivier Pass. At 49km, T-junction left onto N2 George. (If you're skipping Rafikis, stay straight on N2 direct to Knysna.) Turn left to Keurboomstrand at 60km, left again at 62km. At 66km turn right at T-junction. Rafikis is 500m further.

Drink a toast to your day and walk to the looming rock arch at the idyllic Rafikis Restaurant and Bar, above the beach at Keurboomstrand, just outside Plettenberg Bay. Or head back to

GOOD TO KNOW

The Bloukrans Bridge is the world's largest single span concrete arch bridge and it's the third highest bridge in the world (which also makes it the highest in Africa).

Knysna for one more adventure – a sunset cruise through the Heads, with champagne and oysters. There are two operators based at Knysna Quays: if you love the classic lines of a 50-foot yacht, look for Spring Tide Charters and yacht *Outeniqua*, or opt for a spacious catamaran, *Zakat*, from Knysna Waterfront.

Keurboomstrand to Knysna – 30min

Retrace your route from Rafikis. At 4km T-junction turn left to Plettenberg Bay. At 5km T-junction turn left onto N2 Plettenberg Bay. Enter Knysna at 42km. Knysna Tourism is at 45km. (For boat cruises, turn left into Waterfront Drive at 44km, following the signs for Knysna Quays.)

Enjoy dinner at one of Knysna's fine restaurants, but don't make it a late night for you'll need to be up and ready to go quite early the next morning.

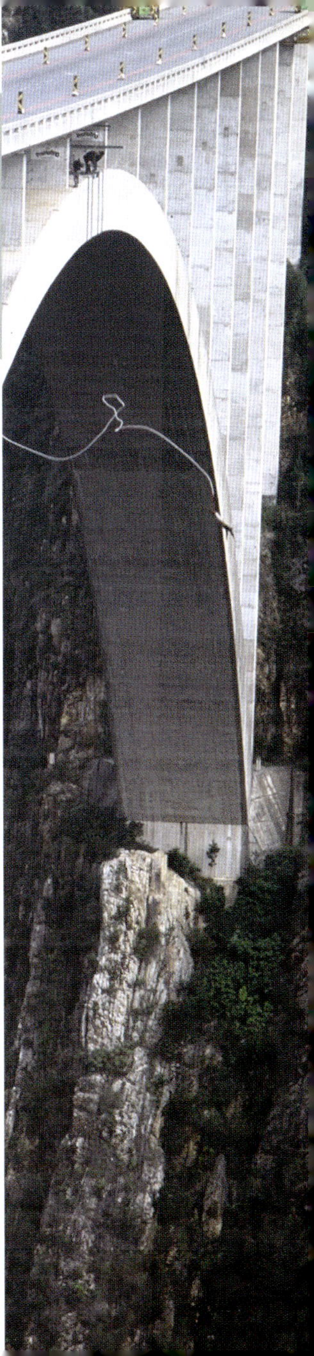

FOUR

Day spent in and around Knysna

The Awesome Foursome is just one of the dynamite packages of non-stop action run by Seal Adventures (depart from Knysna Quays). The half-day starts with paddling a canoe (could be calm and leisurely, could be rough and choppy) from Leisure Island across the lagoon to the Featherbed Nature Reserve on the opposite Head. Then get your boots on, because you're hiking right to the top, with spectacular views of Knysna to take your mind off the strain – just so that you can jump right off it...

No matter how much abseiling you've done before, this one will leave you dry-mouthed. While the actual abseil is 70 metres, your departure point is at the end of a dainty wooden jetty jutting out into thin air, a breathtaking 122 metres above the waves crashing onto the rocks below. Once you've regained your composure – and your breath after the walk back up – you get to do it again, only this time it's face first. You know what they say about not looking down. But when you rap jump, with the rope attached behind you, there's nowhere else to look.

The fourth in the foursome is a quadbike obstacle course that swoops and snakes through the veld on top of the Head, with fabulous views if you're brave enough to take your eyes off the track. Some good advice on quadbiking: 'Steer it like a supermarket trolley and you'll never battle around the corners.'

Come down from the adrenalin high on the gentle walk down to the sea, before canoeing back across the lagoon.

Knysna to Cape Town – 5hrs

It's direct to Cape Town along the N2, or take some extra time and head back on Route 62 via Oudtshoorn (take the N12 at George).

READY TO RALLY?

Instead of storming back down the N2 take a beautifully scenic and exhilarating detour via the Bloukrans and Grootrivier passes which deliver stunning views down into Nature's Valley.

Quadbiking route in the Knysna forest

REGIONAL TOURISM BUREAUS

GARDEN ROUTE AND KAROO REGIONAL TOURISM ORGANISATION
044 873 6314, www.capegardenroute.org

KNYSNA TOURISM 044 382 5510, www.visitknysna.com

MOSSEL BAY TOURISM 044 691 2202, www.visitmosselbay.co.za

PLETTENBERG BAY TOURISM 044 533 4065, www.plettenbergbay.co.za

ADVENTURE OPERATORS

ABSEIL AFRICA 021 424 4760, www.abseilafrica.com

AIR TEAM 082 257 0808, 021 426 0489, www.tandemparagliding.co.za

BIRDMEN 082 658 6710, 021 557 8144, www.birdmen.co.za

CITY ROCK Observatory, 021 447 1326, Mon–Fri 13:00–21:00, Sat–Sun and holidays 10:00–18:00

DAYTRIPPERS 021 511 4766, 082 807 9522, www.daytrippers.co.za

DOWNHILL ADVENTURES 021 422 0388, www.downhilladventures.com, bike tours at 10:00 and 14:00 daily

FACE ADRENALIN 042 281 1255, weekdays 9:00–16:30, 083 264 5221, Gouritz Bridge 044 697 7001, Bloukrans Bridge 042 281 1458, www.faceadrenalin.com

OUT THERE FACILITATION 082 442 5636, www.ventureforth.co.za

TABLE MOUNTAIN CABLEWAY 021 424 8181, www.tablemountain.net
Opening times vary with season, but generally first car up at 8:30 (8:00 in Dec/Jan), last car down 19:00 or 20:00 (22:00 in Dec/Jan)

PARA-PAX 021 461 70 70, www.parapax.com

KNYSNA WATERFRONT SAILING CHARTERS & CATAMARAN CRUISES
044 382 5520, www.knysnaferries.co.za

RAFIKIS RESTAURANT AND BAR Keurboomstrand, 044 535 9813,

Abseiling off Table Mountain

www.rafikis.co.za, daily breakfast, lunch, supper.

SEAL ADVENTURES Knysna Quays, 044 382 5599, 083 654 8755, www.sealadventures.co.za

SHARK AFRICA Mossel Bay, 044 691 3796, 082 455 2438, www.sharkafrica.co.za

SPRING TIDES SAILING CHARTERS (yacht Outeniqua) 082 470 6022, 082 829 2740, www.springtidesailing.com

STORMS RIVER ADVENTURES 042 281 1836, www.stormsriver.com

THE HEADS DIVING ADVENTURE CENTRE Knysna Heads 044 384 0831, Plettenberg Bay 044 533 1158, www.headsadventurecentre.co.za

WILD MOSSEL BAY (adventure bookings) 044 691 3738, www.capegardenroute.co.za

WILD THING Gouritz Bridge 083 299 9900

WHERE TO STAY:

OLD POST OFFICE TREE MANOR Church Street, Mossel Bay, 044 691 3738, www.oldposttree.co.za

SANTOS EXPRESS TRAIN LODGE 044 691 1995

KNYSNA RESERVATIONS 044 382 6960

PHANTOM FOREST ECO RESERVE 7km from Knysna on the Phantom Pass Road, 044 386 0046, www.phantomforest.com

THE POINT Point Road, Mossel Bay, 044 691 3512, www. Pointhotel.co.za

WAYSIDE INN Pledge Square, 48 Main Street, Knysna, 044 382 6011, www.waysideinn.co.za

Golf balls in the rough

THE ROUTE:

It's tee-time at some of the Cape's best courses, from Stellenbosch to Hermanus, then up the Garden Route to Mossel Bay and George.

see MAP A

contact details on pp 230 & 231

TIME: Four days, four nights – the minimum time you'll need for the entire route, but extra time is recommended to make the most of the courses and explore the Garden Route, one of South Africa's most beautiful regions.

DISTANCE: About 500km one-way, and add another 450km for the direct route back to Cape Town on the N2.

BEST TIME TO GO: Summer may dish up a southeasterly wind that ups the golfing challenge. The rain comes in winter, but it's often mild with plenty of good-weather days in between. Autumn is ideal – the holiday crowds are gone, the wind drops and the days are usually pleasant and warm.

golf

INTRODUCTION

Gary Player, Ernie Els, Tiger Woods, Peter Matkovich – we've gone for a celebrity round-up of golf courses in the Cape, on a route that travels to the winelands of Stellenbosch and the Helderberg, dips into some whale-watching territory near Hermanus, then journeys up the gorgeous Garden Route via South Africa's sunniest town. And you get to pit your performance against the world's golfing greats when you play on the links that hosted the Presidents Cup in 2003.

Of course, there's more on offer than just golf – if you can't tell your pars from your putters, there's plenty to keep you entertained too.

This route was put together with Larry Gould, a passionate golfer and former hotelier who has the arduous task of spending long hours chasing small white balls into holes on courses around the country – all in the name of work. Larry also takes golf tours. For more information, visit his website at www.golfincapetown.co.za, or email gouldgolf@global.co.za, or call 021 701 7860. (Guides to golf in other regions are also available.)

READING LIST

✓ Look out for a handy map titled *Guide to Golf in Cape Town and the Western Cape*, at tourism offices, which lists 70 local courses and their contact numbers.

✓ *The Larry Gould Guide to Golf in the Cape*, which describes 38 local courses in detail, is a fabulous source of information to anyone exploring the province with a set of golf clubs in the boot.

Arabella Golf Estate

The 19th hole

THE ROUTE

Day One
• Play at Spier De Zalze and overnight in Somerset West

Day Two
• Scenic drive via Gordon's Bay to Arabella
• Overnight at Arabella, or in Hermanus or Kleinmond

Day Three
• Drive up the N2 and play in Mossel Bay
• Overnight in Mossel Bay

Day Four
• Drive along the Garden Route to George and play Fancourt
• Overnight at Fancourt or in George

BEFORE YOU GO

✓ It's essential to book well before your trip. All the main courses featured here are golfing estates with homes along the fairways. Preference is given to residents and hotel guests before day visitors. We've listed alternative courses in case they are fully booked, but these clubs also experience high volumes, so do phone ahead. Some clubs also have members-only days.

✓ Golf shoes with soft spikes are required on most courses in the Cape region.

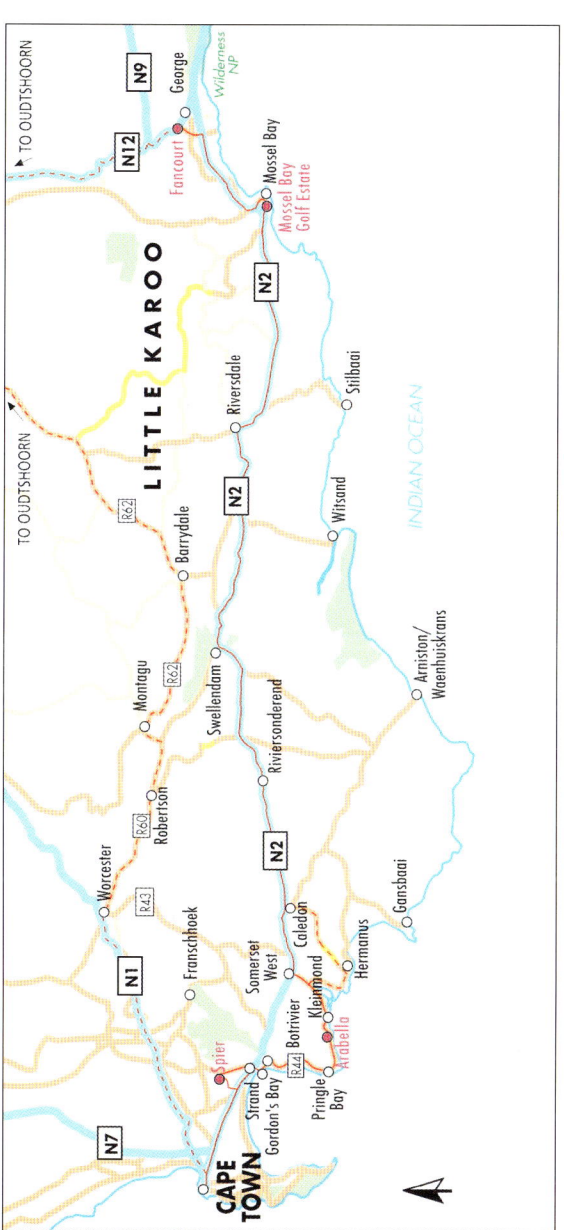

George Golf Club

ONE

Waterfront to
Spier De Zalze, Somerset West – 35min

From the Waterfront turn left to N1 Paarl then follow N2 Somerset West. After about 32km, take Exit 33 Baden Powell Drive, Stellenbosch R310 and turn left at the stop (as if you were going to Spier). Turn right into Annandale Road (at the large strawberry). At the four-way stop turn left onto R44 and continue towards Stellenbosch, then turn left into De Zalze Winelands Golf Club. Spier De Zalze Golf Club, off R44, Stellenbosch: 18 holes, par 72. Type of course: parkland. Length: 5 937m. Clubs, trolleys, drive carts and caddies for hire.

As if there wasn't enough to entertain you at Spier, the De Zalze Golf Club (for now accessed off the R44, not through Spier) issues a unique Winelands challenge – can you finish your round before you succumb to a wine tasting? The course, designed by Peter Matkovich, is unusual in that it meanders through a working farm and vineyard. The result is a spectacularly beautiful winelands experience, with the Stellenbosch mountains as a backdrop to fairways running between vines, fruit trees and lavender, and numerous dams and holes along the oak-lined Blaauklippen River making it one of the Western Cape's most scenic golfing destinations. (And do reward yourself by tasting the Kleine Zalze and Spier wines afterwards.)

Another advantage Spier De Zalze has over many of the other major golf estates is that by embracing tourism, tee times are accessible and visitors are made welcome (club membership is

WHAT YOU NEED TO KNOW ABOUT LOCAL GOLF

- ✓ Because of the type of grass on the greens, divots are not replaced on local courses. Sand is used instead, which allows the grass to knit together again. You can hire or buy sandbags at the clubs.

- ✓ Many local clubs have the very civilised custom of the halfway house – stopping for a 10-minute break for refreshments after nine holes.

- ✓ It's a good idea to use a caddy, available at most clubs. It's customary to tip on top of the official fee, and include something for the halfway house refreshment.

- ✓ Book your self-drive golf carts in advance as they get snapped up rather quickly.

- ✓ Of course we love the 19th hole tradition!

- ✓ And yes, holes-in-one mean an expensive round at the bar here too.

limited to residents). A magnificent new clubhouse overlooks the river, practice area and the 18th green.

Spier De Zalze is due to host the World Amateur Team Championships in 2006, and a new golf village and hotel is also on the cards.

Most challenging hole: 17th par 5 (one of the toughest par 5s in the Western Cape, says Larry) – the fairway curves along the river left of a high bunkered mound, with the river crossing it just before the elevated green.

Where else to play: Somerset West Golf Club – 18 holes, par 73 parkland course (5 928m) crosses a railway line and a road that divides it into three distinct parts. Look out for unusual white squirrels. Or try Strand Golf Club – 18 holes, par 72 parkland course (5 732m). Erinvale Golf Estate – 18 holes, par 72 parkland course (5 892m) is a legendary Gary Player-designed course with two distinct feels. The first nine holes are played on a low, flat part of the estate, while the especially scenic second nine moves up into the rolling high ground, where the hazards are complicated by the slopes surrounding the estates.

When you're not golfing – Somerset West:

- See the Wine and the Kids routes (pp 43–44 & 116) for more info on Spier.
- Historic Vergelegen is beautiful for teas or lunches. Phone the Helderberg Wine Route for more options.
- Visit Helderberg Nature Reserve or hit the beach. See Kids Route (p 123) for more to do.
- Ask Helderberg Tourism about Spookhill, and how you can get your car to roll uphill…

WHERE TO PLAY IN CAPE TOWN

- ✓ There are several excellent courses in Cape Town – these ones each offer something different.
- ✓ Royal Cape Golf Course in Wynberg – 18 holes, par 72 parkland course (5 787m), is South Africa's oldest club and offers international reciprocity.
- ✓ Steenberg Golf Estate in Tokai – 18 holes, par 72 parkland course (6 115m) designed by Peter Matkovich, has you playing in a working vineyard, and you can taste the wine afterwards. (Unfortunately, you need to be staying at the hotel to play the course.)
- ✓ Clovelly Golf Course near Fish Hoek – 18 holes, par 72 parkland course (5 908m) – meanders along a narrow, dune-lined valley stretching from the Silvermine Mountains almost all the way to the beach at Clovelly, take a dip in the warm Indian Ocean after your round. (Saturdays reserved for members only.)

TWO

Spier De Zalze, Stellenbosch to Arabella, Kleinmond – 1hr 15min

Turn right out of Spier De Zalze onto R44 to Somerset West. Cross the highway and continue to Strand. At third lights after Somerset Mall turn right into Beach Road. Turn right at circle, right again at the lights onto R44, Gordon's Bay road. Where the road splits, fork right to Faure Street, signed for Bikini Beach. Follow Gordon's Bay beachfront past the naval base. Turn right at T-junction. Pass Rooiels, Betty's Bay and Kleinmond. Turn right into Arabella about 11km past Kleinmond.

Arabella Golf Estate, on the R44 near Kleinmond and Hermanus: 18 holes, par 72. Type of course: parkland. Length: 6 082m. Clubs, trolleys, drive carts and caddies for hire.

A feeling of great peace will accompany you on this classic, Peter Matkovich-designed course that's been ranked in South Africa's top five. Arabella hugs the Bot River lagoon and rubs shoulders with the Kogelberg Biosphere, South Africa's first internationally recognised biosphere reserve which is regarded as the heart of the Cape Floral Kingdom – the smallest yet most diverse of the world's six kingdoms.

In keeping with that status, Arabella has cleared alien species and planted endemic plants (about four million of them), to create a beautifully natural feel, which recently won them an International Standards Award for environmental management. You will enjoy the wetlands birdlife as well – especially the ornamental pink flamingos.

Each hole is a unique challenge, with the course designed in two large circles so you're not always fighting the wind on gusty days. The layout mixes both long and short par 4s, different directional par 3s and high-risk and reward par 5s, and it's enjoyable for both high and low handicap players. You'll probably use every club in your bag.

Toughest hole: 3rd par 4 – water on the left tempts you to the right, where two strategically placed bunkers lie in wait. The fairway doglegs left to the steeply sloping green, with water on the left to make it more interesting!

Where else to play: Hermanus Golf Club, 18 holes, par 73 parkland course (5 741m) has beautiful tree-lined fairways. Look out for its resident troop of baboons.

When you're not golfing – Hermanus:
- Succumb to absolute pleasure in Arabella's Altira Spa.
- See the Whale Route (pp 181–186) for more nearby options.

THREE

Arabella to Mossel Bay – 3hr

Turn right onto the R44. After about 2km, T-junction left onto R43 Villiersdorp (N2). At about 8km, turn right R43 Bot River, Villiersdorp, Caledon (N2), and join the N2 Caledon. Remain on the N2 until Mossel Bay, at about 303km. Follow golf signs right into 11th Avenue, left into 21st Avenue, then right into 17th Avenue.

Mossel Bay Golf Estate, 17th Avenue, Mossel Bay: 18 holes, par 72. Type of course: links. Length: 5 763m. Caddies available for hire.

Mossel Bay has gained a reputation as a 'must play' course when you're in the area, not only for challenging golf – the greens can be ferociously quick at times – but because how many other courses can boast that you can see the sea from every tee? The course is high up on the hill above the town and the sweeping fairways are flanked by fynbos. There's little on the flat, some tees are high above the fairways, while some greens are well above the landing areas of the holes. Mossel Bay's other claim to fame is that it has the third highest number of sunny days in the world! But, being on a headland, the wind can up the ante on blustery days.

Most memorable hole: 3rd par 4 – at almost 400 metres only the long hitters can do it in two, especially into the wind. The tee is high above the target, the fairway running downhill to the green (with rough and well-placed bunkers on either side), all against the deep blue of the Indian Ocean.

Where else to play: There is a nine-hole course at Boggomsbaai, near Dana Bay and Vleesbaai, outside Mossel Bay. The first nine holes of a Peter Matkovich-designed course at Pinnacle Point near Mossel Bay are due for completion at the end of 2004. Dolphin's Creek golf course in Great Brak is a mere 20 minutes away.

When you're not golfing – Mossel Bay:

- Mossel Bay is famous for its beaches, and whale watching at Cape St Blaize Cave, near the lighthouse at The Point.
- You can see four of the Big Five (sadly no elephant) at Botlierskop Game Farm (20 minutes from Mossel Bay), or go game-viewing on a quad bike at Zingela Indlela.
- See Adrenalin Route (pp 205–207) and ask Mossel Bay Tourism for more info on activities such as shark diving, parasailing, scenic flights and helicopter trips.

FOUR

Mossel Bay to Fancourt, George – 50min

Leave Mossel Bay following signs for N2, George. At about 39km take Exit 425, R404 George Airport and Herold's Bay. Turn left and pass airport. Continue straight over R102, following signs for Oudtshoorn, Blanco. Fancourt is 8km from the N2.

Intricate design makes for interesting golf

Fancourt Hotel and Country Club Estate, Montagu Street, Blanco, George: Four 18-hole courses: The Montagu, The Outeniqua, The Links and Bramble Hill. Clubs, trolleys, drive carts and caddies for hire.

Ernie Els calls it home, Jack Nicklaus says it's the best links he's ever encountered, and Gary Player has said: 'Fancourt is the best golf resort on the planet. There is nothing in the world that compares – nothing.'

Fancourt hosted the Presidents Cup in November 2003, so be prepared for world-class facilities and exceptional manicuring on the greens and fairways, all set below the spectacularly beautiful Outeniqua mountains on the Garden Route. The Montagu has been voted the number one golf course in South Africa, while The Outeniqua is often a blaze of colour. On The Links you can pit yourself against the Presidents Cup performances. Bramble Hill is the newest course open to day visitors (The Montagu and Outeniqua are for residents or hotel guests only), offering sloping fairways in hilly terrain with some rather tricky water hazards to trip you up.

Best hole-in-one hole: 2nd par 3 on The Montagu – well, it's where Larry Gould did it! The target is visually well below the tee, with a creek on the right and three barely visible pot bunkers on the left. The green lies on a sharp rise backed by a bunker.

Where else to play: George Golf Club is an 18-hole par 72 parkland course, voted one of South Africa's top 10 layouts. It's gorgeously green and lush, with the purple Outeniqua mountains as a backdrop.

When you're not golfing – George:

- Board the Outeniqua Choo Tjoe, a historic steam train which puffs between George and Knysna daily, except Sundays.
- Explore Knysna, or see the Adrenalin Route (pp 206–212) for more info.

George to Cape Town – 5hr

Drive directly back to Cape Town along the N2, or take an extra night or two and head back on Route 62 via Oudtshoorn (take the N12 at George).

View over Erinvale Golf Estate

GOLF COURSES

ARABELLA COUNTRY ESTATE on the R44 near Kleinmond, 028 284 9383, www.arabella.co.za

BOGGOMSBAAI GOLF COURSE near Mossel Bay, 044 699 1163

CLOVELLY GOLF COURSE Clovelly Road, Clovelly, 021 782 1118, www.clovelly.co.za

DALTON'S CREEK GOLF ESTATE Great Brak, 044 620 3278

ERINVALE GOLF ESTATE Lourensford Road, Somerset West, 021 847 1144, www.erinvale.co.za

FANCOURT HOTEL AND COUNTRY CLUB ESTATE Montagu Street, Blanco, George, 044 804 0000, www.fancourt.com

GEORGE GOLF CLUB CJ Langenhoven Street, George, 044 873 6116, www.georgegolfclub.co.za

HERMANUS GOLF CLUB Main Road, Hermanus, 028 312 1954, www.hgc.co.za

MOSSEL BAY GOLF ESTATE 17th Avenue, 044 691 2379

ROYAL CAPE GOLF COURSE 174 Ottery Road, Wynberg, 021 761 6551, www.royalcapegolf.co.za

SOMERSET WEST GOLF CLUB Rue de Jacqueline, Somerset West, 021 852 2925, www.somersetwestgolfclub.co.za

SPIER DE ZALZE GOLF CLUB off the R44, Stellenbosch, 021 880 1996, www.spier.co.za

STEENBERG GOLF ESTATE Tokai Road, Tokai, 021 713 2233

STRAND GOLF CLUB Beach Road, Strand, 021 853 6268

ALL THE REST

ALTIRA SPA AT ARABELLA 028 284 0000

BOTLIERSKOP GAME FARM 044 696 6055, www.botlierskop.co.za

HELDERBERG NATURE RESERVE 021 851 4060

Fancourt Hotel and Country Club Estate

VITAL INFO

HELDERBERG WINE ROUTE 021 852 6166

OUTENIQUA CHOO TJOE 044 801 8288/202

ZINGELA INDLELA 044 694 0011, www.greatbrakriver.co.za/zingela

REGIONAL TOURISM BUREAUS

HELDERBERG TOURISM 186 Main Street, Somerset West, 021 851 4022, www.helderbergtourism.co.za

HERMANUS TOURISM Old Station Building, Mitchell Street, 028 312 2629

MOSSEL BAY TOURISM Market Street, 044 691 2202, www.visitmosselbay.co.za

GEORGE TOURISM 124 York Street, 044 801 9295 (reservations 044 801 9299), www.georgetourism.co.za

GARDEN ROUTE AND KAROO REGIONAL TOURISM ORGANISATION 044 873 6314, www.capegardenroute.org

KNYSNA TOURISM Main Street, 044 382 5510, www.visitknysna.com

WHERE TO STAY:

BEACH HOUSE ON SANDOWN BAY Kleinmond, 028 271 3130, www.relaishotels.com

DIE OU PASTORIE Somerset West, 021 852 2120, www.dieoupastorie.co.za

DOLPHIN BAY HOTEL Mossel Bay, 044 691 9001, www.dolphinbay.co.za

ERINVALE ESTATE HOTEL Somerset West, 021 847 1160, www.erinvale.co.za

FANCOURT HOTEL George, 044 804 0000, www.fancourt.com

MUNRO MANOR Mossel Bay, 044 691 3440, www.munromanor.coza

THE VILLAGE HOTEL Spier Estate, 021 809 1100

VILLA MARI GUESTHOUSE Mossel Bay, 044 691 2130

THE WESTERN CAPE HOTEL AND SPA – ARABELLA COUNTRY ESTATE and THE ALTIRA SPA 028 284 0000, www.arabellasheraton.com/westerncape

GLOSSARY

Baobab: Huge 'upside-down' trees found in Limpopo Province and further north in Africa

Bergie: A vagrant

Boerekos: General term for Afrikaner-type, country-style food

Dassie: The rock hyrax

Fynbos: A general term for the distinctive Cape vegetation of shrubby species with fine, hard leaves

Kapenaar: Person of the Cape

Mampoer: Strong spirit distilled from wild fruit

Ouma: Grandmother

Padstal: Roadside farm stall

Perron: Afrikaans for railway platform

Potjie: A stew prepared in a three-legged cast iron pot over an open fire

Renosterveld: Vegetation that predominates in the Swartland

Sandveld: Generally fynbos on inland sandy plains

Shebeen: A township tavern or pub

Spaza: A roadside stall, usually in a township, selling anything from cigarettes and chocolate to cooldrinks and cellphones

Strandloper: ('beach walker') Name coined by early Dutch settlers in the Cape for indigenous tribes that lived off the sea

Strandveld: Coastal thicket or vegetation

Veld: 'The bush', or open areas of natural vegetation

Vel(d)skoen: an ankle-length boot of soft but strong rawhide

Witblits: Home-made brandy, usually high in alcohol content

PICTURE CREDITS

3RD i GALLERY

SHARON PEERS happily combines her career of running a gallery with that of photographer, relishing the stimulation afforded to alternate the hats of both creator and director. In so doing, she has consciously chosen to create her work, as well as give it a mouthpiece with which to share her passion.

Having completed a B.A. Social Sciences through Unisa, Sharon chose to pursue a career in art and her fascination with the philosophical, psychological, social and spiritual aspects of human nature is reflected in all aspects of her life and work.

Sharon's photographs feature worldwide in projects by leading interior designers and architects. She has participated in numerous group shows and has held two solo exhibitions. Visit her gallery, Framing co. inc. 3RD i GALLERY, to see more of her work. See the Art and Desirables Route on p 106 for more information.

INDEX

237

MAP B

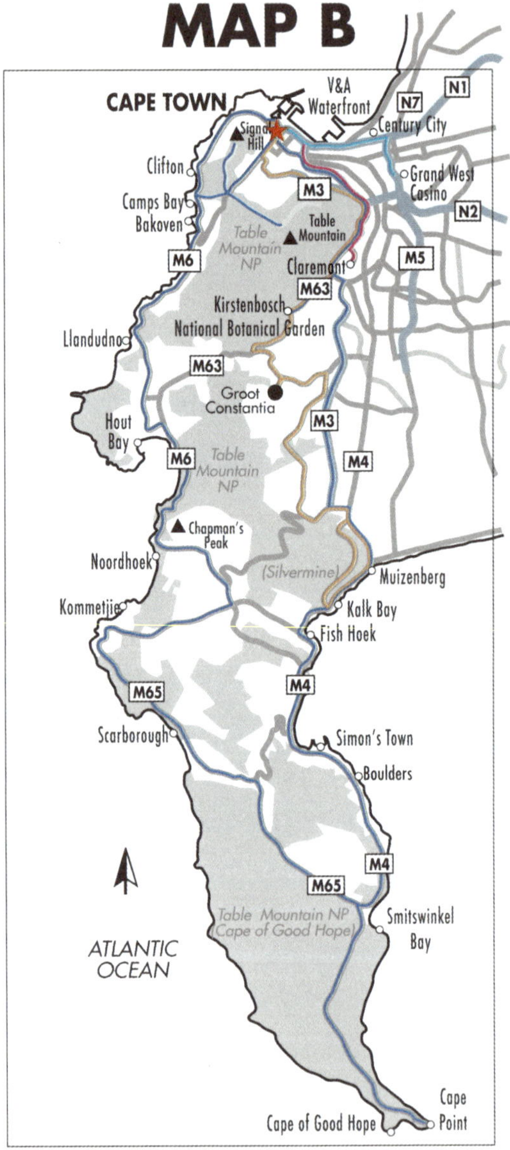

CAPE TOWN

V&A Waterfront

N1

N7

Century City

Signal Hill

Clifton

M3

Camps Bay

Bakoven

Grand West Casino

N2

Table Mountain NP

Table Mountain

M6

Claremont

M5

M63

Kirstenbosch National Botanical Garden

Llandudno

M63

Groot Constantia

M3

Hout Bay

M4

M6

Table Mountain NP

Chapman's Peak

(Silvermine)

Noordhoek

Muizenberg

Kommetjie

Kalk Bay

Fish Hoek

M65

M4

Scarborough

Simon's Town

Boulders

M4

M65

Table Mountain NP (Cape of Good Hope)

Smitswinkel Bay

ATLANTIC OCEAN

Cape of Good Hope

Cape Point

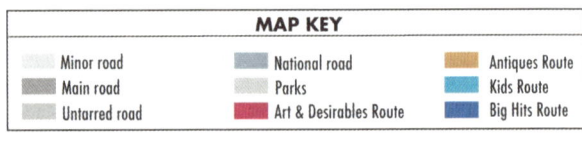

MAP KEY

Minor road	National road	Antiques Route
Main road	Parks	Kids Route
Untarred road	Art & Desirables Route	Big Hits Route